Images of War

LUFTWAFFE BOMBERS
IN THE BLITZ

Andy Saunders

Pen & Sword
AVIATION

First published in Great Britain in 2015 by
PEN & SWORD MILITARY
an imprint of
Pen & Sword Books Ltd,
47 Church Street,
Barnsley,
South Yorkshire,
S70 2AS

Copyright © Andy Saunders, 2015

A CIP record for this book is available from the British Library.

ISBN 978 1 78303 0 224

The right of Andy Saunders to be identified as the Author of this Work has been asserted by him in accordance with the Copyright, Designs and Patents Act 1988.

All rights reserved. No part of this book may be reproduced or transmitted in any form or by any means, electronic or mechanical including photocopying, recording or by any information storage and retrieval system, without permission from the Publisher in writing. Printed and bound in Malta by Gutenberg Press Ltd

Pen & Sword Books Ltd incorporates the Imprints of
Pen & Sword Aviation, Pen & Sword Maritime,
Pen & Sword Military, Wharncliffe Local History, Pen & Sword Select,
Pen & Sword Military Classics and Leo Cooper.

For a complete list of Pen & Sword titles please contact
Pen & Sword Books Limited
47 Church Street, Barnsley, South Yorkshire, S70 2AS, England

E-mail: enquiries@pen-and-sword.co.uk
Website: www.pen-and-sword.co.uk

Contents

Acknowledgements 4

Introduction 5

Chapter 1 – London's Burning! 9

Chapter 2 – Not All Returned 39

Chapter 3 – New Year, Same Story 77

Acknowledgements

The photographs contained in this volume are largely from my private archive of images that I have collected of Luftwaffe aircraft downed in Britain during the period 1939 to 1945. A great many friends and colleagues have assisted me in the quest for these photographs, or otherwise provided additional information. In no particular order of merit, I would like to thank:

Peter Cornwell, Steve Hall, Chris Goss, Dennis Knight, Winston Ramsey, Phillipa Hodgkiss, Alfred Price and Martin Mace.

In addition, I must mention two other fellow researchers who are no longer with us but who's work added considerably to our sum of knowledge relating to the recovery of aircraft wrecks in wartime Britain. They are my late friend Pat Burgess and a colleague of many years, Peter Foote. Pat had been a prodigious collector of information relating to the county of Sussex, the area in which much of the activity described in this book had taken place. Peter Foote had been equally industrious in recording the minutiae of events during the Battle of Britain and the Blitz across Britain since the late 1940s and his tireless research work has left a legacy of unequalled information. Had he not recorded some of these events before it was too late to find the evidence then our knowledge of that period would be much the poorer. In many cases, he put considerable historical detail and context to photographs that would otherwise have been a rather less informative record of the momentous events they depicted.

Lastly, I feel I should mention the late Kenneth Watkins. Ken was a collector of Luftwaffe aircraft crash photographs and after his death I was fortunate to be able to acquire his large collection. Ken's photographs complemented and added to those already in my own archive but I was able to extensively draw upon that resource in compiling this book.

In addition, I must extend my thanks to any other individuals and organisations who may have assisted me in over forty years of research and whom I may have inadvertently overlooked. My thanks to you all.

Introduction

Whilst German air attacks on mainland Britain started in October 1939, and to a greater or lesser extent on its towns and cities, it is generally considered that the 'Blitz' began on 7 September 1940 and continued through to the spring of 1941. Unlike the Battle of Britain (10 July 1940 to 31 October 1940) the Blitz has no *official* commencement and cessation dates. It is accepted that the assault began on 7 September 1940, but its end date was rather less definite. The Luftwaffe air assault on Britain's cities just petered out as German efforts turned eastwards towards Russia in Operation Barbarossa. For the purposes of this book, however, the 31 May 1941 has been taken as the cut-off point for the end of the Blitz, because it corresponds with a significant reduction in Luftwaffe raids. Air attacks of a much more limited nature continued pretty much unabated until almost the end of the war in Europe, but never again in such strength as the raids from September 1940 to April 1941.

The word 'Blitz' is short for *Blitzkreig*, literally lightning war, the word that had been applied to describe the German assault on Poland in 1939 and on France and the Low Countries in 10 May 1940. But it also became the word used to describe the bombing raids on British cities. Of course, 7 September 1940 was also a date that fell during the height of the Battle of Britain and, in reality, the commencement of the Blitz was just a development of Luftwaffe tactics in the air war against Britain. Initially the Battle of Britain had seen attacks on coastal convoys and ports, and then the focus of attack was switched to RAF airfields before this gave way to all-out raids against cities, towns and industrial centres. Initially, these operations were round-the-clock, with the night bombers being guided to their targets by fires stoked during the daylight attacks, and the raids increasingly took a heavy toll on civilian targets.

As with the Battle of Britain, so the Blitz saw its various distinct phases as the Luftwaffe changed its *modus operandi* to suit tactical requirements and, indeed, in response to operational lessons that were being learned. For example, it quickly became apparent that the daylight raids, even when they were heavily escorted by fighters, remained vulnerable to the still strong defensive organisation that was RAF

Fighter Command. A weakness in the aerial defence of Britain, though, could be exploited during the hours of darkness since RAF night-fighting was yet in its infancy and anti-aircraft guns were so inaccurate that they were not a significant factor. However, as the night Blitz gathered pace so the impetus for development and implementation of more effective defensive measures gained momentum and by November 1940 the first successful interception using airborne interception radar (A.I.) resulted in the destruction of a German bomber over land. This event might be considered perhaps the beginning of the end of the Blitz, for the virtual cloak of invisibility that the darkness of night had afforded the German raiders had been lifted. All the same, until RAF night fighting defences (and, later, radar controlled anti-aircraft guns) had got into their stride, the best chance of survival for Luftwaffe bombers remained the night-attack, and by October 1940 the daylight raids had all but ceased. All but ceased, that is, apart from a new innovation that came that autumn: the fighter bomber.

By October the Luftwaffe were sending formations of Messerschmitt 109s carrying single 250kg bombs in attacks mostly against London and in formations that were, in turn, protected with fighter cover provided by other Me 109s. But the operations during October and November of 1940 very much heralded the development of the German's fighter-bomber (or Jabo) units which would later cause so much havoc, principally in south coast and southern English towns.

As the Blitz continued on into the late autumn and winter of 1940, so the number of towns and cities being attacked widened throughout the length and breadth of Britain. Notable amongst them was Coventry, attacked with devastating results on the night of 14 November 1940. Inexorably, the night raids continued throughout the winter of 1940/41 and on into the early spring, but given the weight of numbers involved in the aerial assaults the numbers of aircraft actually being brought down was not high. Nevertheless, there were casualties aplenty as the attacks came almost night after night so far as weather conditions would permit.

Speaking at the start of the London Blitz on 7 September 1940, Reichsmarschall Hermann Göring set the scene in a radio broadcast, thus:

'I now want to take this opportunity of speaking to you, to say this moment is a historic one. As a result of the provocative British attacks on Berlin on recent nights the Führer has decided to order a mighty blow to be struck in revenge against the capital of the British Empire. I personally have assumed the leadership of this attack, and today I have heard above me the roaring of the victorious German squadrons which now, for the first time, are driving toward the heart of the enemy in full daylight, accompanied by countless fighter squadrons. Enemy defences were, as we expected, beaten down and the target reached. I am certain that our successes have been as massive as the boldness of our plan of attack and the fighting spirit of our crews deserve. In any event, this is a historic hour in which for the first time the German Luftwaffe has struck at the heart of the enemy.'

The die had been cast. London and Britain's other major towns and cities were about to endure many months of ordeal by fire.

It is not my intention to comprehensively tell the story of the Blitz in this book. Instead, the purpose is to give a glimpse of those deadly days and nights through photographs of some of the aircraft lost during attacks against this country, images of the crews involved and examples of the damage they wrought, as well as taking a brief look at some of those who strove to defend the night skies of Britain during that momentous period when the whole country faced all that the Luftwaffe could throw at it.

Andy Saunders
East Sussex, May 2014

Chapter 1
London's Burning!

When the Luftwaffe launched its all-out assault on London and other British cities on 7 September 1940 it marked a turning point in the war, and in warfare generally. Moving away from its campaign throughout the Battle of Britain, which had targeted mostly military and industrial targets, the attacks in what became known as the Blitz rained death and destruction onto Britain's primary cities, especially London. Of course, there was an industrial and commercial element to these attacks rather than just being random or wholesale bombings of residential areas. In a sense, the damage wrought on residential areas was almost collateral damage since the primary objectives were docks and industrial installations. That said, it was certainly not an unintended consequence of these raids that saw destruction among the huddled housing of dock workers and other 'key' employees who lived adjacent to their places of employment. The disruption this caused, not to mention the impact upon morale, was certainly intentional. In this chapter we primarily look at the effect this bombing had on the cities, their infrastructure and their buildings, and upon the people who lived there and who had to endure the merciless onslaught of the Luftwaffe.

At first, the attacks came by day but this ran on into the first night of the Blitz and then, first daily and nightly, and after just nightly, for over eight months. The whole face of Britain's cities, and some of its provincial towns, were altered forever and the scars left behind are still visible to this day. These, though, are the visible scars and for many still living today there remain the mental and emotional scars of the period and the still tangible sense of loss suffered by whole communities and individual families. It was a time of terror, but also one of extreme fortitude and outstanding valour. These elements shine through in every one of the images presented in this chapter.

They called it 'Black Saturday'. On this day, 7 September 1940, the Blitz proper began on London by the Luftwaffe. It was the commencement of an almost continual day and night bombardment of the Capital that lasted 257 days until 21 May 1941. Of the attacks that began on 7 September, the Inspector General of Air Raid Precautions, Wing Commander John Hodsoll, noted: 'It was indeed an awe inspiring sight that met our eyes. Huge clouds of black smoke were billowing and spiralling into the clear blue sky; great spurts of flame were shooting up; there was the dull thud of bombs as they exploded and reverberated in the distance, and an acrid smell of burning was borne on the wind. The docks looked as if they had been reduced to one great inferno.' This was the view seen that momentous day by Hodsoll as the docks beyond Tower Bridge were turned into a raging inferno. Some called it the Second Great Fire of London.

Across the city, smoke and flames from the raging inferno could be seen rising across the East End of London. This photograph was snapped illicitly out of a bedroom window near Sydenham Hill during the late afternoon of 7 September 1940. Witnesses could scarcely believe what they were seeing as the Capital seemed increasingly engulfed in fire.

Nearer to the centre of the action, this photograph was taken from Fleet Street as the fires took their inexorable hold in dockland. The image of St Paul's Cathedral rising unharmed above the destruction became a symbolic icon of The Blitz and emblematic of the fortitude and national solidarity that stood against the Luftwaffe's assault. Remarkably, St Paul's survived the horrendous bombardment that took place all around it, although not entirely unscathed.

Whilst it was principally the commercial assets of the London Docks that fell into the German bomb sights that day, it was inevitable that surrounding residential properties should suffer. Indeed, the death, displacement and demoralisation of the workers who lived there was all part of the German plan. In these huddled streets lived those who worked in the docks and its associated industries, and here the toll was heavy. This was the scene in Stepney Way on Sunday, 8 September – the morning after the night before. What the stunned inhabitants did not know was that this was just the beginning.

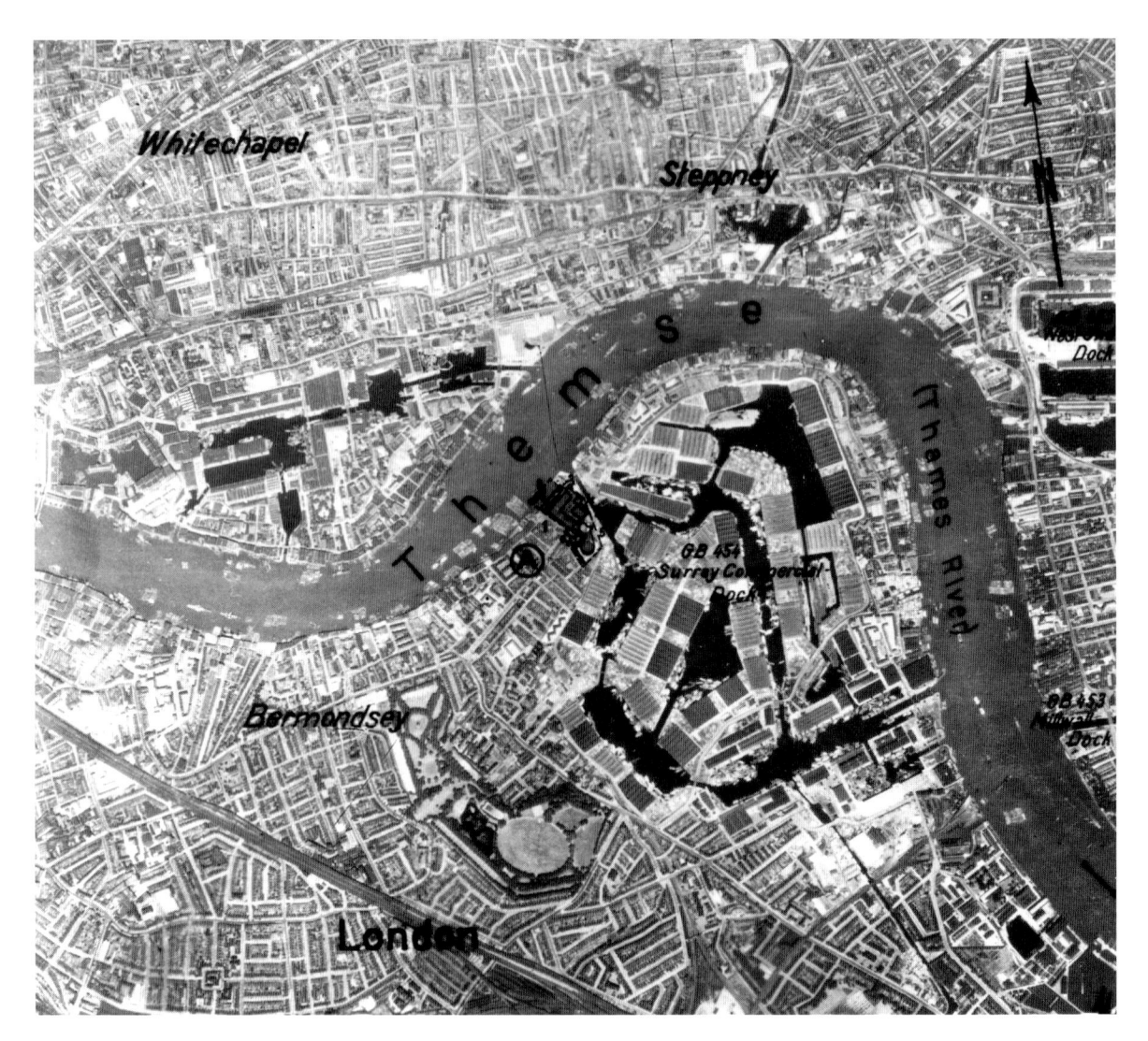

This was how German aerial reconnaissance of the area appeared in 1940, with this photograph showing the East End's Surrey Docks highlighted and the West India Dock and Millwall Dock highlighted on the other side of the River Thames. Stepney Way (previous page) runs just to the left of the 'S' of Stepney annotated on this image.

A little further eastwards down the Thames, at the Shell Mex BP Works on the northern bank of Thames Haven, the oil storage tanks were attacked and set ablaze during the late afternoon of Saturday 7 September 1940. Clearly, this was a prime target for the Germans and the blazing tanks were photographed by the Luftwaffe once the fires had taken hold there.

The majority of these Luftwaffe target or post-strike photographs were taken by single high-flying Dornier 17-P photo-reconnaissance aircraft. Lightly armed, with a crew of three, the aircraft relied upon altitude and speed to evade interception and brought home highly detailed photographs for analysis.

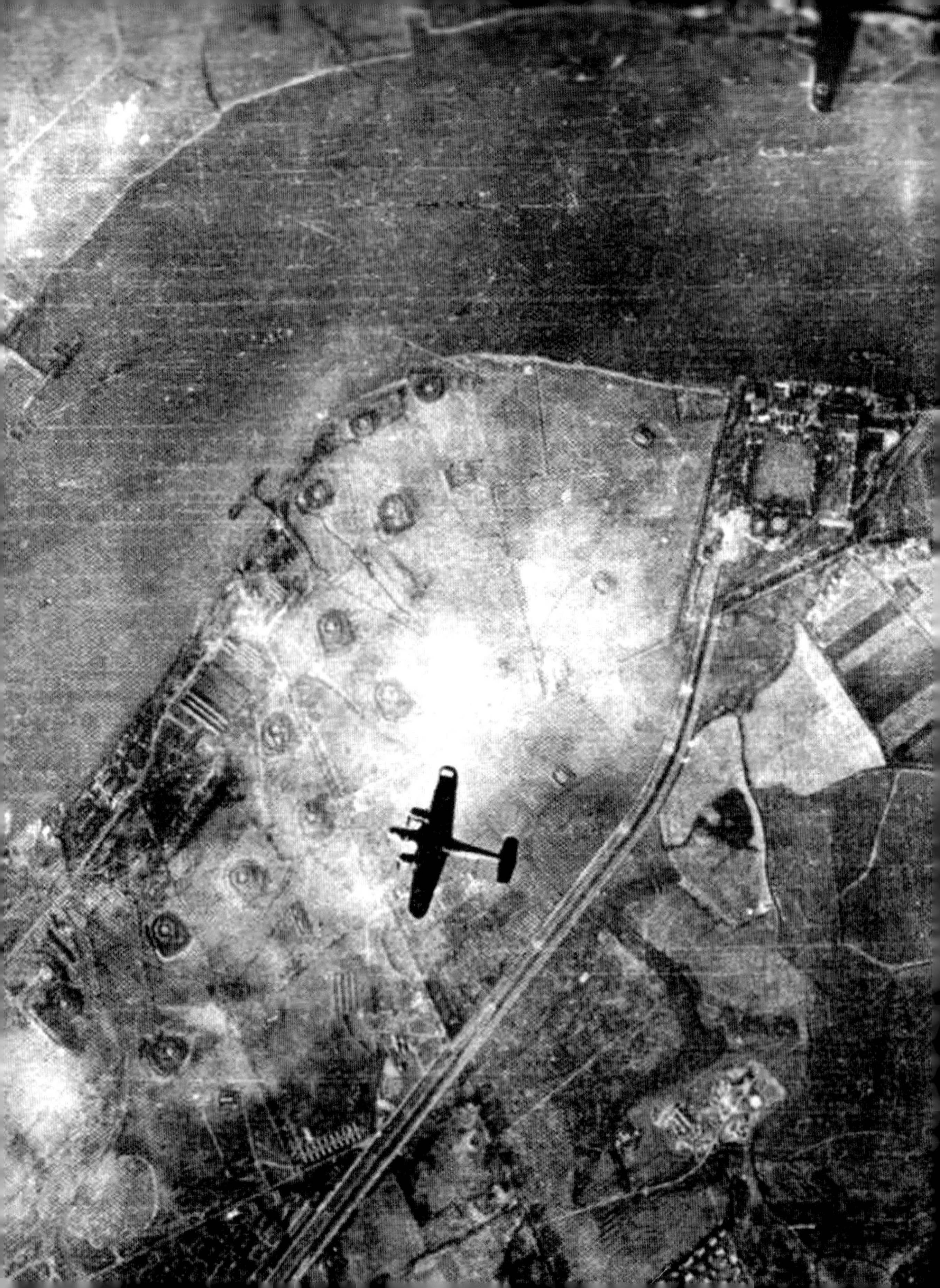

Left: But it was the Dornier 17-Z bomber, with its crew of four, which made up much of the backbone of the Luftwaffe bomber force operating against London during the summer and autumn of 1940. Here, a formation of Dornier 17-Z bombers overflies what is now Thamesmead, near Woolwich, on the afternoon of 7 September 1940, photographed from another bomber flying in a higher formation.

Below: And from the ground, this was the formidable sight that almost daily presented itself to the civilian population during September 1940: a high flying formation of the same Dornier 17-Z bomber aircraft. High above them, and often unseen, weaved the escorting Me 109 and Me 110 fighters ready to pounce on any intercepting RAF fighter aircraft. The approaching drone of massed formations of Luftwaffe bombers was often the portent of destruction faced by those who endured the Blitz.

With the fires stoked up during the day, so the Luftwaffe bombers returned after night-fall in further attacks against the already blazing city, the flames from the huge and growing conflagration being clearly seen by the enemy raiders as soon as they crossed the French coast. Whilst high explosives shattered docks, quaysides and associated infrastructure, and blasted huddled dwellings, so a rain of incendiary bombs showered across the scene of destruction. These small 1kg devices were dropped in clusters, and could quickly cause devastating results as fires took hold in residential areas and industrial complexes. Here, an incendiary bomb flames in a London street on the night of 7 September 1940. A sign in the background points the way to an air raid shelter and the white rings painted on trees and lamp posts aid visibility during the black out.

Right: The incendiary bomb menace was a major issue during the Blitz, especially with the bombs smashing through the slated roofs of houses and setting light to the stored contents of lofts. Householders were exhorted to empty lofts and have buckets of sand and shovels ready. This was a commonly-seen public information poster of the period.

Beat 'FIREBOMB FRITZ'

BRITAIN SHALL NOT BURN

BRITAIN'S FIRE GUARD IS BRITAIN'S DEFENCE

ISSUED BY THE MINISTRY OF HOME SECURITY

Amidst all the mayhem of falling bombs, the anti-aircraft defences of London added to the din and commotion as gun batteries around the city blasted away into the night sky. Their successes were perhaps somewhat limited given the number of aircraft overhead, although at this stage of the war the RAF's night fighting defences were yet woefully inadequate. To an extent, the AA fire helped public morale with the feeling that at least some 'fighting back' was underway. On the other hand, the exploding artillery shells showered their own deadly splinters widely across the city, often causing death and injury below and also damaging property. Here, the anti-aircraft guns in Hyde Park are shown in action, at night, during 1940.

Heading up the Army's Anti-Aircraft Command was General Sir Frederick Pile. Prime Minister Winston Churchill urged him to: 'Keep on shooting away, regardless'.

Shaken by the first raids of the Blitz, Winston Churchill visited the East End of London on the afternoon of 8 September to see for himself the damage that had been inflicted. Amongst the places he visited was the burnt out shell of the Silvertown Rubber Company factory on the junction of Winchester Street and Factory Road. As his car later picked its way through the rubble-strewn streets and headed back to Downing Street, so the bombs began to fall around them in dockland.

Taken at night, by the brilliant incandescent light of burning buildings, a six-storey warehouse in the docks blazes out of control and illuminates like day all of the other buildings around it. As a rather futile fire hose plays into the total loss that this warehouse has become, white flames and embers from the stored contents shoot almost a hundred feet into the air and act as a navigational beacon to more and more incoming bombers. Popular stories told of it being possible to read a newspaper in far-away Kent or Sussex by the light from the blazing city. Often, water pressure was too low due to fractured mains and a supply had to be pumped direct from the Thames. The hose, here, seems to not be producing a particularly powerful jet.

The assault went on day and night through most of September, with commercial and industrial sites around the East End being the principal targets. Here, Thames-side warehouses are ablaze at St Katherine Docks as a London Fire Brigade fireboat jets water into the flames in a futile attempt to stop the spread of fire. Meanwhile, other bombs and incendiaries rained down around the docks and fuelled the huge blaze that had become the second Fire of London. The song from the first great fire, 'London's burning, London's burning, fetch the engines, fetch the engines, Fire! Fire!, Fire! Fire! pour on water…', sung with much fun by schoolchildren across the years, rather belies the true horror of this widespread blaze, in this case stoked up by a constant rain of high-explosive.

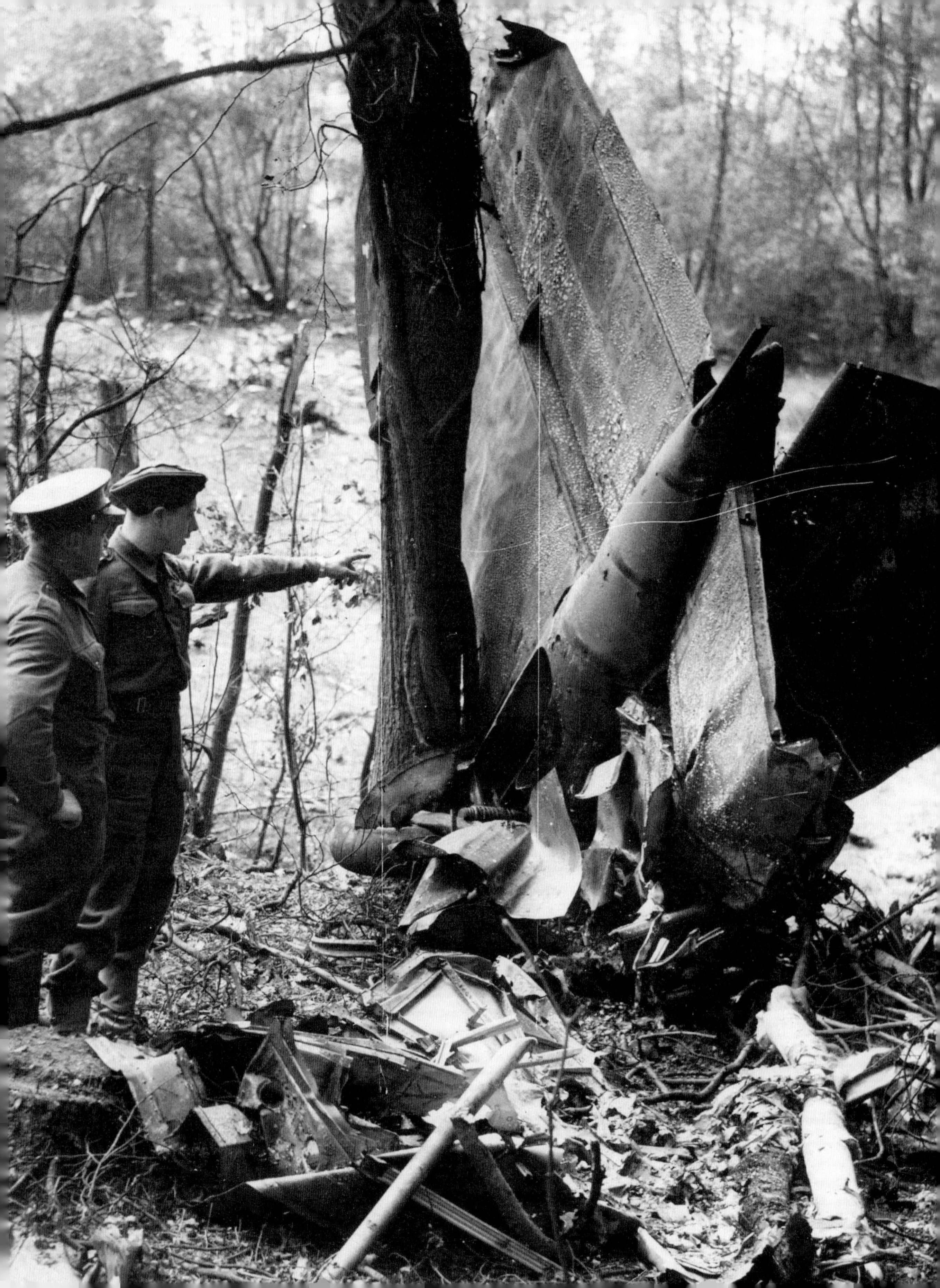

Left: Despite the relative paucity of effective defence against night bombers, at least during the early part of the Blitz, a Heinkel 111 of 3./KG4 on a raid against London was caught in a searchlight beam north of RAF North Weald and spotted by a patrolling RAF Blenheim night fighter of 25 Squadron. Closing on its quarry, the Blenheim managed to send the bomber crashing to earth at Down Hall to the east of Harlow. Two of the crew baled out into captivity, the other two being killed. Here, military personnel inspect the charred tail section of the German bomber.

The wreckage at Down Hall attracted quite a collection of military sightseers who are seen here with two local ARP Wardens as one of the badly damaged engines comes under scrutiny for the benefit of the camera. The aircraft was on its run-in to London, but dumped its bomb load once the RAF Blenheim had attacked.

Those travelling into the city to begin work on the morning of Monday, 9 September 1940 found the familiar surroundings they had left on Friday, 6 September changed forever. Buildings and landmarks had been shattered, burned out or had totally vanished whilst the air was heavy with the smell of burning, the smog of acrid smoke and a gentle fall of ash. Meanwhile, the debris-strewn streets were festooned with miles of fire hoses.

Apart from the docks themselves, and the adjacent residential accommodation, the rail infrastructure of London suffered badly during the Blitz. Here, work gets underway to repair damage inflicted around Battersea during the mid-day attacks of Sunday, 15 September 1940, traditionally marked as 'Battle of Britain Day'.

Again, the huddled trackside houses also took a pounding and these near **Battersea** have suffered considerable blast damage from a heavy calibre bomb which has disrupted the permanent way and blasted a deep crater.

Bridges and viaducts could be the most difficult structures to quickly repair. Disrupted rail track could be lifted, craters filled and new rails fitted quite rapidly but bridges and viaducts often required a greater level of engineering to repair them. Travel into London today by rail and you will often see different coloured patches of brickwork from repair work, or even the marks left by flying bomb splinters. Given the scale of the assault it is little wonder that plenty of visible evidence still exists today.

Nur für den Dienstgebrauch

Bild Nr. 684 SK 74

Aufnahme vom 24. 9. 39

Zielgebiet II London

Maßstab etwa 1 : 18 800

Genst. 5. Abt. Oktober 1940

GB 54 1 a London - Westham, Abwasseranlagen Northern Outfall Sewers, Abwasserpumpwerk Abbey Mills (s. auch Zielgebiet I)
  50.97   ,,   , Kraftwerk Westham
  50.98   ,,   - Bow,   Bow
  52.28   ,,   - Bromley, Gaswerk Bromley
  52.47   ,,   , Leven Road

Left: One of the targets marked out for attack on 15 September 1940 was the Bromley-by-Bow gasworks which is marked by a thick black line in the almost dead centre of this Luftwaffe reconnaissance photograph and annotated at the bottom of the image. The gas works were very heavily hit that day. Although this target photograph is dated October 1940 it appears to have been taken prior to 15 September as no damage is yet evident.

For the very large part, it was London that was taking the major brunt of the Blitz raids but that is not to say that other towns and cities were immune from German attack. Far from it. Here, a scene of utter devastation has been wrought on the area around Woolston railway station near Southampton. Again, this was on 15 September 1940.

A little further west from Woolston, the Royal Navy base at Portland came under attack from the Heinkel 111s of III./KG55 and among the units taking part was the 8th Staffel of that KG55 formation. Although we cannot know if he specifically took part in that raid, Lt Hans Thurner (seated here at the controls) of an 8./KG55 He 111 became one of the most highly decorated Luftwaffe bomber pilots of the war and took part in the Battle of Britain and The Blitz. In this posed photograph he is seen with his Great Dane dog and two crew members. Thurner's luck finally ran out when he was killed on 11 June 1944, despite the lucky horseshoe hanging in his cockpit.

It was also on 15 September 1940 that St Paul's Cathedral was delivered from its greatest threat of the Blitz: an unexploded 1,000 kg bomb buried beneath the cathedral clock tower. It had been dropped there during the early hours of the 12 September, at 02.25 hours. Because of the risk to the cathedral the decision was taken to dig out the bomb and, hopefully, dispose of it safely. Meanwhile, across several days, all routes to the cathedral were barred as 16/17 Section Bomb Disposal Company dug down over twenty-seven feet to reach it. Here, a lonely policeman bars the way up Ludgate Hill as digging work goes off to the right of the clock tower and just out of view.

On 15 September the bomb was finally recovered by a party under the command of Lt Robert Davies and driven to Hackney Marshes where it was exploded. Here, the clear up work commences by the St Paul's steps and workmen prepare to mend a ruptured gas main. The flames from the leaking gas caused initial complications until it could be turned off and the fire extinguished.

During the daylight attacks, RAF Fighter Command had the capability to intercept the incoming raids and did so through the early stages of the Blitz with varying degrees of success. Often, the RAF fighters were in the right place at the right time to disrupt the attacks, but it was almost always the case that at least some of the bombers would get through. Those that got close to the city, or overhead, would also meet a barrage of anti-aircraft fire, day and night, as we have seen on page 20. This was 52 Heavy Anti-Aircraft Battery with its 4.5inch guns at Barking, Essex, ready to engage raiders approaching up the Thames Estuary.

Whilst London was the principal target immediately after 7 September 1940, other cities were on the target list and increasingly so later in 1940 and on into the 1941. Many other provincial towns came under regular and sometimes sustained air assault. A case in point was Eastbourne, on the East Sussex coast, which by the time the war ended had become the most raided coastal town. This was the aftermath of a raid there on 28 September 1940 when bombs fell at the junction of Cavendish Place and Tideswell Road.

Peggy Harland, a young victim of the Luftwaffe bombers, was posthumously awarded the Girl Guides Gilt Cross for Bravery.

Rescue workers toil in the debris to pull out the dead and injured. In total, three people were killed and fourteen injured. One of the injured was 17-year-old Peggy Harland who was trapped for many hours under debris and eventually an amputation of both legs had to be made in order to free her. Cheerful throughout her dreadful ordeal, Peggy eventually succumbed to her injuries two days later. Her rescuers toiled relentlessly, despite the nearby presence of an unexploded bomb, and many of the party received gallantry awards and commendations; three won the George Medal, and another the MBE.

Towards the end of September 1940 the mass daylight raids en masse gradually petered out and gave way, largely, to nocturnal raids. This raid that hit London's Tottenham Court Road came overnight on 24/25 September. The devastation was typical of that which was now being inflicted on a widespread scale across the city.

This was Austin Friars, not far from the Bank of England, after being hit during a night raid in October, and as firemen clean up the following morning. This depressingly familiar scene increasingly greeted Londoners as they emerged from overnight shelter, often having taken cover in London Underground stations.

The penultimate in this series of images showing what the Luftwaffe bombers inflicted on London during the Blitz of 1940/1941. It depicts the scene in Balham High Street on the evening of 14 October 1940. A bomb had penetrated the Northern Line Underground and caused flooding in the tunnel, with water and sewage cascading into the tubeway. The bomb also caused this bus to plunge into the huge crater but, remarkably, the driver escaped with only minor injuries. However, sixty-eight people died in the underground station where many were taking shelter. The London Underground was not always the safest place to take shelter during air raids.

After another overnight raid, this was the scene in Leicester Square on the morning of 17 October 1940. Even the skills of the Automobile Association, whose HQ stand behind the wrecked vehicles, would have been hard-pressed to get any of these back in running order! Truly, London had burned day after day and night after night. But it had not been without cost to the Luftwaffe bombers.

Chapter 2
Not All Returned

As the Luftwaffe onslaught intensified in its fury, so the losses incurred by the attacking forces began to multiply. In this chapter we look at some of those casualties through images of the tangled aircraft wreckages or faces of the young German crew members.

Whilst effective defence against night raiders was in its relative infancy during the early days of the Blitz there were, nevertheless, significant losses being sustained – although not all of these were directly the consequence of the defender's actions. Sometimes, they were down to navigational errors or just plain accidents. All of them, though, resulted in the loss of German crews as either casualties or POWs if they were downed over Britain. However, some managed to make it back home, albeit in damaged aircraft or with injured, dead or dying crew men. Looking back now, and even though they were the enemy intent on the subjugation of Britain by brutal means, it is sometimes difficult not to feel a pang of compassion for these young men who were, after all, serving their country. They, too, certainly shared the terror and the fear of those they were attacking. Very often they ended up paying the price and frequently died in horrific circumstances. That said, their attacks on British cities may well have lit the firebrand that escalated this total warfare to such an extent that, later, RAF Bomber Command and the USAAF would reciprocate damage upon German cities – but on a scale that left the attacks of the Blitz looking almost insignificant by comparison. The wind had certainly been sown, and the whirlwind would surely be reaped in the fullness of time.

As 1940 ended, so the attacks continued into 1941 although, by now, the objective of eliminating Britain as an effective fighting power as a prelude to invasion had been somewhat revised and the plans put on hold. Now, as the New Year approached there was certainly to be more of the same for London and many other towns, cities and industrial centres. However, 1940 had left its mark of destruction; shattered communities and a trail of wrecked Luftwaffe machines and broken bodies of crew members strewn the length and breadth of Britain.

Amongst the raiders attacking London on 8 September, and coming to stoke up the fires created by the Luftwaffe over the previous twenty-four hours, were groups of Dornier 17-Z bombers of KG 2. Here, crews of that unit wait by their aircraft for the order to go. Some didn't return to their home airfield that day.

Over Farningham, Kent, two aircraft of 5./KG 2 took hits from anti-aircraft fire and crashed. One of them literally exploded in mid-air, although a single crew member escaped by parachute. Of the other aircraft, all four men baled out into captivity. This is most likely the wreckage of the Dornier that exploded in the air and fell in pieces around Farningham Road Railway Station, with the undercarriage being one of the largest portions to fall to earth.

The defensive efforts of RAF Fighter Command inflicted a steady attrition on the Luftwaffe bomber force during its daylight offensive, which began to drain its very lifeblood. While losses were not yet at a wholly unacceptable level, the high casualty rate eventually prompted a switch to an almost entirely night offensive. One of the daylight losses on its way to target at the London Docks was this Junkers 88 of Stab.II/KG 30 shot down and burning at Court House Farm, Barcombe, East Sussex.

Of its crew, one was killed and the other three were taken prisoner. Oblt Hans-Gert Gollnisch, the pilot, later told his story: 'The target could already be seen when our aircraft was hit by a very short burst of fire from a British fighter that had approached below us, unseen. Our aircraft was badly damaged and there was no response from the control column. Both engines were damaged; the left one losing oil and the right one losing petrol. Then one of my crew reported that the rear gunner, Uffz Ernst Diebler, was lying dead in a pool of blood, a bullet having pierced the artery of his neck. I dropped our bombs and somehow managed to make a forced landing in a meadow. I was very lucky to manage it because all around there were obstacles of all kinds, placed there to prevent landings by German glider troops.' Gollnisch was indeed lucky, but for him and his two surviving crew members the war was over, and 22-year-old Ernst Diebler had paid with his life.

Another of the Junkers 88 London raiders from KG 30 was this aircraft of the Staff Flight shot down not too far away at Newells Farm, Nuthurst, during the same sortie. Despite the battered state of their aircraft all four crew members were captured unharmed. The local newspaper of the period spoke triumphantly of: '…another Nazi raider who won't be coming back to London with its cargo of terror!'

Two days later, on 11 September, and another raid aimed at London's Commercial Docks saw stiff resistance and some heavy losses sustained by the Heinkel 111 bombers of KG1 and KG26. This was one of the He 111s of 6./KG 1 that was forced down through fighter action at Camber, East Sussex, where its crew set fire to their aircraft before being taken into custody. The poles to obstruct landings by enemy assault gliders, which Oblt Gollnisch mentioned, can be seen planted widely across the fields.

As we have seen, although the emphasis shifted to night raids, mass daylight attacks against industrial and commercial targets other than London were still being mounted by the Luftwaffe up until late September 1940. This was the Heinkel 111 of 1./KG55 shot down by Hurricanes of 238 Squadron during an attack on the Bristol aeroplane factory at Filton, Bristol. It carries an impressive raging bull emblem on its fuselage, but it was RAF Fighter Command who saw the red rag when this mass attack on 25 September raged across the West Country. The Heinkel finally came to grief at Studland, Dorset. Four of its crew were captured, and a fifth died later in hospital.

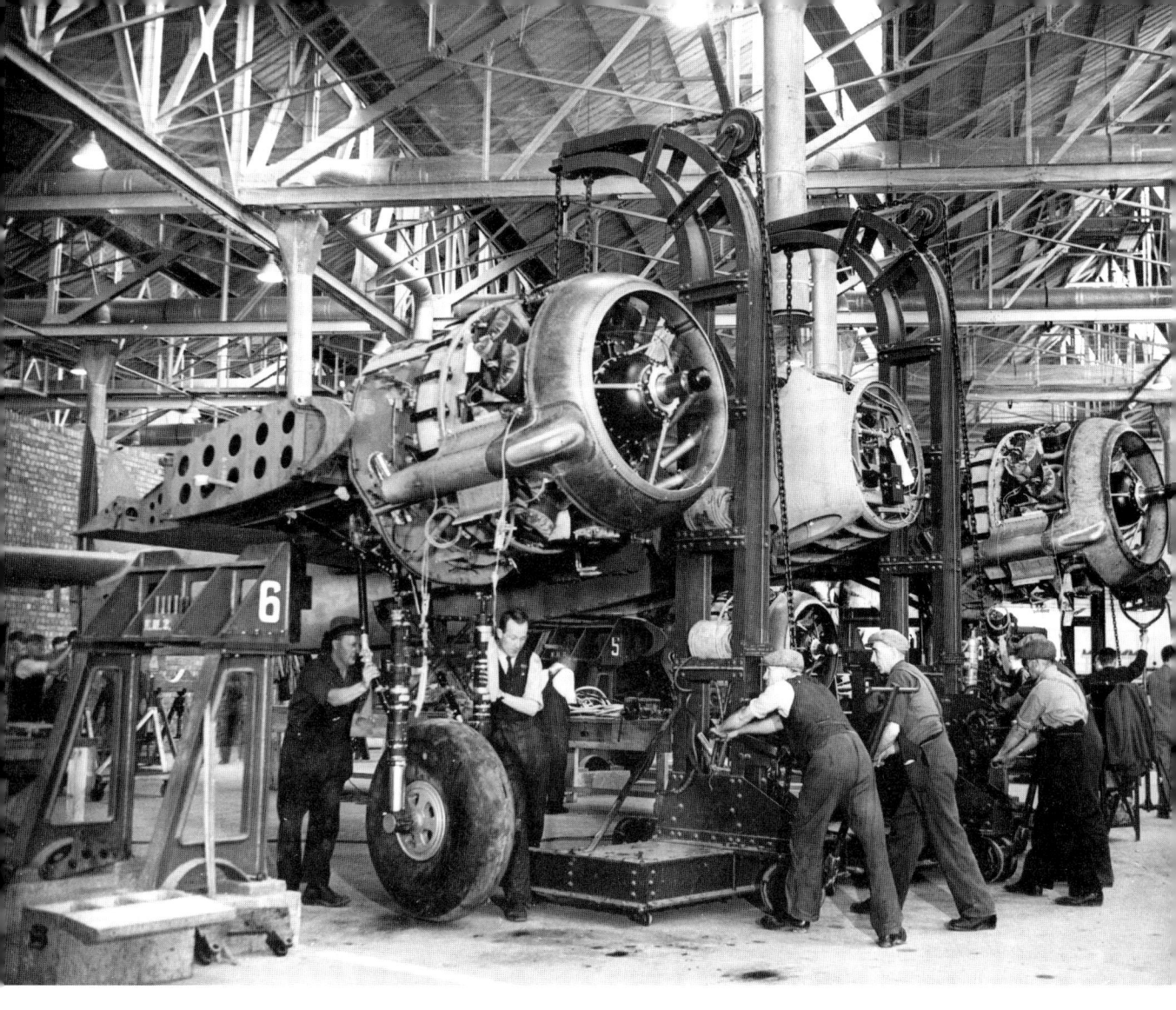

The Filton works were, among other things, constructing the Bristol Beaufighter which was then just coming on-stream with RAF Fighter Command as a successful night-fighter aircraft countering the Luftwaffe night Blitz. Its effectiveness was greatly enhanced with the introduction of Airborne Interception Radar (or AI) that was also just coming on-stream. Targeted attacks on factories such as these, and the potential disruption to the supply of new fighters reaching the RAF, could obviously strike a massive blow were they to succeed to any extent.

By Friday, 27 September 1940 mass escorted daylight raids on London and other targets were coming to an end. It was a day that also saw its share of Luftwaffe losses, among them this Junkers 88 of 1./KG77 that was hit and shot down by anti-aircraft fire at around 11.05 hours on the run in to its London target. All of the crew baled out, although one died when his parachute failed to open. The wreckage broke up and spread itself around about the Angas Home for Aged Seamen at Cudham, Kent. As ever, the wreck attracts the attention of the Police, the Military and civilians.

It is possible that those who came to investigate, to guard or just to gape at the smashed up bomber may have been unaware of the fact that its bomb load was still on board. After all, this was an aircraft that was inbound to its target. In this photograph the object standing left foreground is, in fact, a set of fins from a 500 kg bomb. The Policeman at right seems blissfully unaware of any potential danger!

The Junkers 88 had broken into three distinct portions; forward fuselage, centre section with engines, and the tail assembly. Here, the severed and inverted tail lies some distance from the main wreckage.

Yet another Junkers 88s of KG77, this time from 2./KG77, was shot down at Folly Farm, South Holmwood, Surrey, earlier that same morning. It was also headed for London, but the crew jettisoned their bombs before baling out. Three of the crew landed safely but one man, Uffz Wilhelm Menningmann, fell out of his parachute harness and plummeted to his death at the Leatherhead Sewage Treatment Works. The unfortunate Menningmann suffered a fate that most British citizens of the period doubtless felt he deserved. Perhaps a reflection of that feeling was the sad spectacle of Menningmann's lonely funeral, reputedly attended by only the priest, the pall bearers and the undertakers. Very often, such funerals had a wide military presence, conducted with military honours, and with attendant groups of civilians who were either curious or caring. If the story is correct, then this all seems to have evaporated for Willi Menningmann who still lies buried in Leatherhead Cemetery. Here, fire fighters deal with the smoking crater caused by the violent vertical impact.

Uffz Rudolf Schumann was the pilot of the Junkers 88 downed at Folly Farm. Here, he poses confidently in front of his qualification as pilot, prior to being taken into captivity.

Probably less confident, and doubtless shocked and frightened, was **Uffz Hans-Joachim Tenholt**, the observer, who is seen here being bundled into an army car shortly after his capture.

Meanwhile, soldiers from the unit who captured Hans-Joachim pose with their battle trophies: his Mae West lifejacket and gathered-up parachute.

Although the massed daylight raids were drawn down, there continued to be sporadic activity during daylight hours by the Luftwaffe bomber force. This was generally un-escorted, mostly conducted by singleton aircraft or very small groups, and often of little value militarily. Although this aircraft, a Junkers 88 of Stab I./KG 77, was a lone raider shot down on Thursday, 3 October 1940 its attack had an unintended although successful outcome for the Luftwaffe. Trying to find Reading, the crew became lost in poor visibility and accidentally stumbled upon the de Havilland aircraft factory at Hatfield. Here, the crew executed an accurate attack that killed twenty-one factory workers, injured another seventy, and destroyed eighty per cent of the materials and work in progress for the new Mosquito bomber. It was a significant blow to an important military aircraft project. The airfield defences were alert, though, and put up a barrage of machine gun and 40mm Bofors gun fire which hit and crippled the Junkers 88. The bomber crash-landed in flames at Eastend Green Farm, Hertingfordbury, where the crew scrambled clear and were captured unharmed before the fire took hold.

51

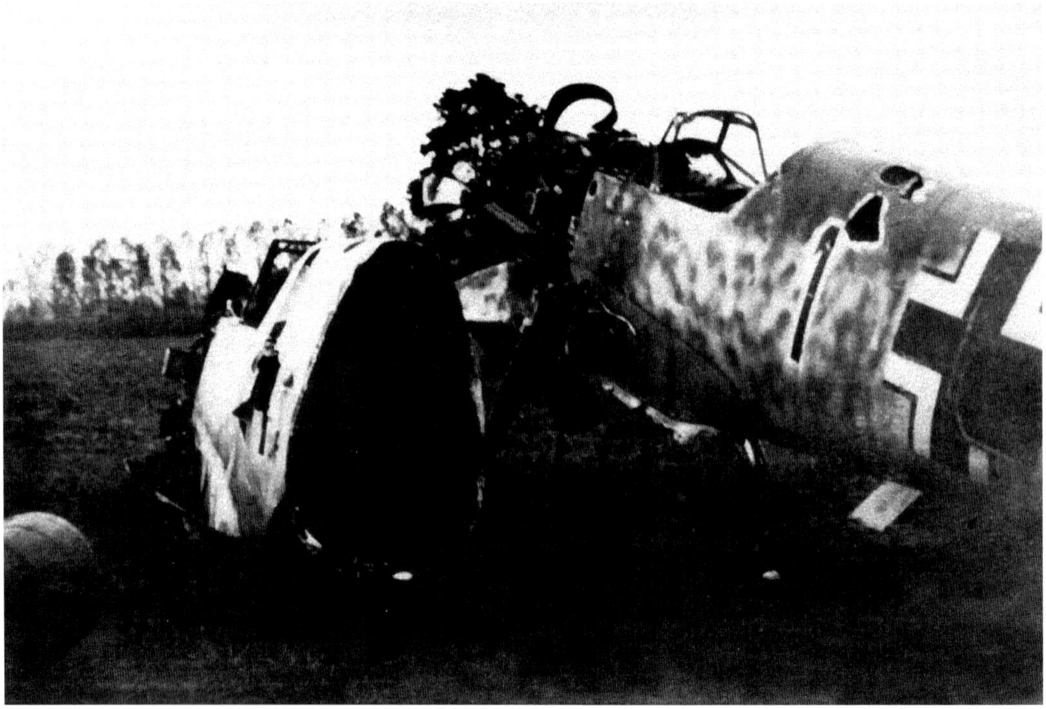

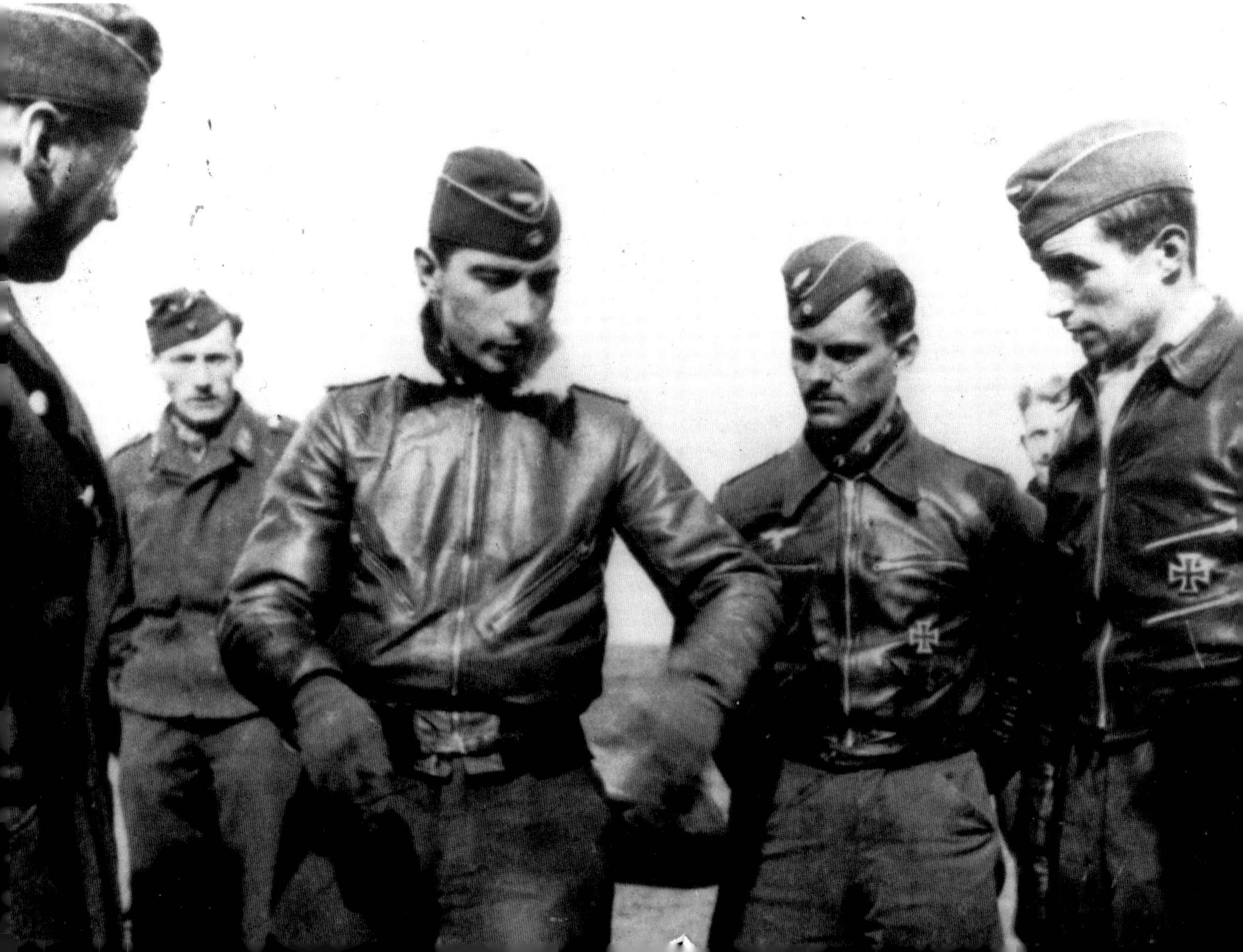

Top Left: A new innovation during October 1940 was the introduction of the Messerschmitt 109 fighter-bomber to daylight raids, principally in attacks against London. These aircraft, escorted by other Me 109s purely in the fighter role, carried out attacks with a single 250 kg bomb. On 7 October 1940, Oblt V Molders, brother of the famous fighter ace Major Werner Molders, was part of a raiding force from 2./JG 51 attacking the docks when he was hit by RAF fighters and brought down, making a forced landing at Guestling, to the north of Hastings. This was his Messerschmitt 109 photographed later in a scrap processing depot. The fighter-bomber attacks became a feature of the Blitz during the autumn of 1940.

Bottom Left: Oblt Victor Molders (right) listens as his brother Major Werner Molders (left) explains tactics. On 7 October, 1940, Victor flew his last mission and later told of his experiences that day: 'That morning my brother asked me to fly a mission. My Staffel, eight aircraft, were armed each with a 250 kg bomb. We took off from Pihen and climbed to 18,000 ft towards London where we were to attack the docks to disrupt the unloading of shipping. We were protected by my brother's section and eight other fighters. In order to make a better strike we flew over in attack formation, and then went very low on the run-in. We were almost between the roof tops of the city. It was funny to see the flak bursting above me! Then, my brother reported that the escort would have to return home because they were getting low on fuel. Shortly after, somebody shouted 'Indians behind you!' and looking up I saw about thirty Spitfires above and diving down on us. All I remember is being hit in the radiator and in total my Messerschmitt took thirty-two bullet strikes, I'm told. Now, my coolant had all escaped and before long my propeller turned no more. Looking behind, I saw a lone RAF fighter behind me and then he flew alongside me, waved, and broke away. I never saw him again. I was too low to bale out and so I began to look for a suitable field to land but all of them were covered in obstacles like old cars and tall poles. I eventually had to crash on the bank of a ditch, and did so successfully. The aircraft showed no signs of burning, and so I set my maps on fire with my cigarette lighter and tried to burn my aeroplane, but it failed. Shortly afterwards, three Home Guard men captured me and one of them said 'Spitfire is better than Messerschmitt' and I said 'No, Messerschmitt is better!' Then I felt a warm feeling on my boot and looked down to see that a dog had peed on me! I was taken for breakfast at a farmhouse, then off to a Police Station where I flushed my notes on the mission down the toilet. When I was taken for interrogation by the RAF they thought they had captured my famous brother, and when they found it was just me they were very disappointed!'

It became a tradition for the ground crews of the Me 109 fighter-bombers to chalk messages to their enemy on the bomb casings. Although this one is obscured, it is fair to assume it was of either a rude or a jocular nature; and signed 'Uncle Hugo'.

Another bomb has a message which reads, 'Dear Tommy, hearty greetings from Hein[rich], with the wish: it must be hit!'

Another sneak raider, heading for the important city of Liverpool, was this Junkers 88 of 2./KGr806 that was shot down during the late afternoon of 8 October 1940. The aircraft flew low past RAF Speke, just as three Hurricanes of 312 Squadron were being scrambled to intercept, with Flt Lt D E Gillam opening fire on the bomber whilst taking off and with his undercarriage still down! Hit, the aircraft went down, to make a forced landing at Bromborough Dock, Port Sunlight, with its bomb load scattered randomly around its landing path. One crew member was dead, two others were wounded and only one was captured unhurt. The destruction of this bomber was thought to have been the fastest aerial victory of the Second World War, with under three minutes from take-off, to victory, to landing. The unit emblem, an eagle gripping an iron cross, is splattered with bullet hits.

One of the Junkers 88's 250 kg bombs lies in the foreground as crowds of sightseers begin to gather. According to the *Birkenhead Advertiser* of 12 October 1940 the battle, and the crashed bomber itself, was 'A tonic sight for hundreds'. The same page, reporting attacks on 'an industrial quarter' also went on to note: 'It is officially announced that up to September 15th there were twenty-six recorded cases of enemy aircraft machine-gunning civilians in this country, and several cases have occurred since.' As the Blitz on Britain had amply demonstrated, this was total war and the civilian population was very much in the front line.

Right: The cockpit of the Junkers 88 at Bromborough Dock is inspected by local RAF men from RAF Speke. It was here, in this seat, that Lt zur See Heinrich Schlegel was killed in a hail of bullets from RAF fighters. The relatively cramped accommodation for four men on board the Junkers 88 is evident in this photograph.

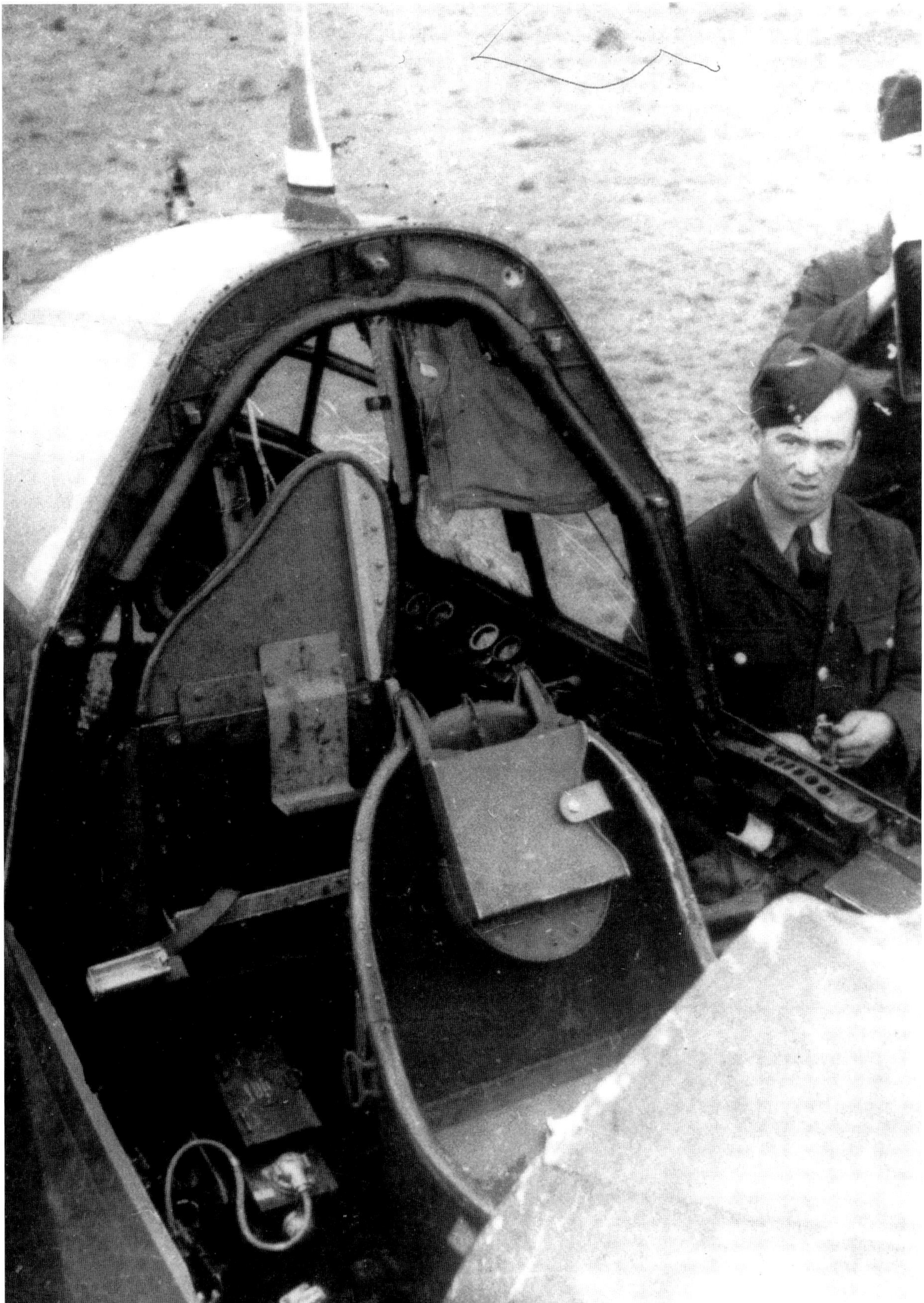

Apart from Luftwaffe bombers that were actually shot down over the British Isles during the Blitz period a great many struggled back, damaged, to their French bases whilst others simply vanished in either the North Sea or the English Channel. This is a Heinkel 111 of KG 55 that made it back to France after a night sortie to London, finally ending up making a creditable landing in a field.

This Heinkel 111 of 8./KG 55 ended up in rather a worse state after a landing incident at its home airfield of Villacoublay, and Ofw Bernhard Hickel and his crew were lucky to survive. A Flammenbombe (250 kg incendiary device) had failed to release over the target and fell out of its stowage on landing, with this result.

Ofw Bernhard Hickel, pilot of the burned out-out Heinkel.

Other losses over 'home' territory had less fortunate results for the crews involved. This Heinkel 111, also of **KG 55**, disintegrated in flames when it ploughed into woodland near its home base, killing all of the crew. Only the burnt-out tail survived relatively intact to show that this was once a Heinkel.

This Luftwaffe airman is holding propeller blades salvaged from the same wreckage, possibly in order to later place them on the flier's graves. This was a regularly observed honour afforded by airmen to their fallen comrades.

Meanwhile, the lone raiders continued to ply their trade and although on a late afternoon attack on 27 October 1940 this Junkers 88 of 7./KG4 wore a somewhat nocturnal emblem: a silver bat against a yellow moon. Although the Luftwaffe was attacking RAF airfields during the summer of 1940 their targeting had, principally, moved away from such locations. However, this aircraft had been on a low-level attack against RAF Linton-on-Ouse when it was engaged by ground fire and crashed at Richmond Farm, Duggleby, Yorkshire. Three of the crew were captured unharmed, but **Uffz Oskar Piontek** was severely wounded and died of his injuries on 15 November 1940.

Shortly before 8 pm on the evening of 16 October 1940 a Junkers 88 of Stab II./KG 30 crashed beside the A119 road at Much Hadham, Essex, for reasons unknown. The aircraft was carrying its full bomb load, and the high-explosive cargo and fuel tanks exploded violently, this being the result. Parts of the aircraft and its unfortunate four occupants were scattered far and wide, leaving a difficult and unpleasant clear-up task for the authorities.

Initially presenting something of a mystery for investigators, this Dornier 17-Z of 1./KuFlgr.Gr606 made a perfect belly-landing on mudflats at Ewarton, Suffolk, near the Royal Navy shore base of HMS *Ganges* on the night of 21/22 October 1940 – the only problem was that there was no trace whatsoever of the crew. It transpired that, on a night sortie to bomb Liverpool, they had become lost and baled out over Salisbury Plain. The pilotless aircraft flew on for over 130 miles before landing itself on the mudflats. Meanwhile, the crew were all rounded up in Wiltshire, and the Police and military authorities there mounted a search for the crashed aircraft the German airmen had abandoned!

Coventry is a name synonymous with the horrors of the Blitz, and whilst this crash of a Dornier 215 B photo reconnaissance aircraft at Eaton Socon happened before the bombing of that city it was, nevertheless, connected to it. The aircraft, of 3./Aufkl.Gr.Ob.d.L, was on a sortie to Coventry around mid-day on 24 October 1940 when it was intercepted by three Hurricanes of 1 Squadron and its engines set alight. All four occupants baled out, but the parachutes of three of them failed to deploy. The fourth was captured very badly injured. Meanwhile, the Dornier smashed itself to pieces across fields near the Crown Inn. The Luftwaffe would have to wait for a re-run of this failed reconnaissance sortie, although the Coventry operation was already very much in the planning.

It was Birmingham that was primarily raided on Friday, 1 November 1940 although Coventry was also struck that night. It was a Birmingham raider that came to grief at Greyfriars, Storrington, West Sussex. Hit over Birmingham, this Junkers 88 of Stab I./LG 1 struggled back as far as the South Downs but then flew into the rising ground in the dark, apparently when attempting a forced landing. Three of the crew died; the fourth survived and was taken prisoner.

This is the same scene, photographed the next morning. When James Waller, away serving in the army at the time, saw the pictures of this crash in the newspapers, it caused him quite a shock. At once he recognised the location: his back garden!

A fighter-bomber sortie by the Messerschmitt 109s of 9./JG 26 on 5 November 1940 ended in catastrophe for the ace fighter pilot Staffelkapitan who was leading the sortie: Oblt Heinz Ebeling. Crossing the coast near Dungeness he collided with another aircraft in the same formation flown by Uffz Wilhelm Braun. Both men parachuted to safety, but soldiers later posed with the crumpled wreckage of Braun's Messerschmitt and particularly displayed its bomb rack for the camera.

Hit by anti-aircraft fire, a Heinkel 111 of 2./KG 1 broke apart in the air and fell across houses at Johnson Road, Bromley, on the night of 9 November, 1940. One civilian, a Mrs Alice Monday, was killed and another six people were trapped. Remarkably, Lt Max Probst escaped from the bomber by parachute, although his three colleagues were killed.

Police Sgt David Grigg and Dr Kenneth Tapper were both awarded the George Medal for courage shown during rescue work in the collapsed buildings and among unexploded bombs that were scattered in the wreckage of the aircraft and rubble.

The cache of 50 kg bombs lined up in Johnson Road, Bromley, after being de-fused by RAF bomb disposal specialists. In the background, a contingent of tin-hatted Police officers assemble. Could that be the heroic Sgt Grigg on the right of the photograph?

It was another Junkers 88 of LG 1, this time the 8th Staffel, that got caught on one of the solitary daylight missions that were so often proving fatally dangerous for Luftwaffe bomber crews. This aircraft was shot down at around 14.00 hours on 13 November after being sighted over Coventry and chased by Spitfires of 611 Squadron. The Coventry connection, on this date, was perhaps significant given that it was the very eve of the devastating and infamous attack on the city. The crippled aircraft finally made a wheels-up landing at Woodway Farm, Blewbury, Oxfordshire, where three of the crew members were captured by a Special Constable and a Home Guardsman. The fourth man, Gefr Bossdorf, had been killed in the attack by 611 Squadron's Spitfires.

Buried locally this was **Gefr Hans Bossdorf's** original grave marker, provided by the Imperial War Graves Commission. Generally, deceased German service personnel who died in the British Isles were buried in consecrated ground in local cemeteries and churchyards but very often, as here, they were buried away from other graves and on the edges of burial grounds so as not to offend local sensibilities. Bossdorf was exhumed from this location in the late 1950s and re-buried at German Military cemetery, Cannock Chase.

Right: Coventry. The very name still evokes thoughts of the terrible night of 14 November 1940, when massive and sustained raids involving hundreds of Luftwaffe bombers pounded the city. The raids were devastating and resulted in massive destruction, the deaths of 568 people, 863 seriously injured, and 393 with lesser injuries. It also resulted in the destruction of Coventry Cathedral which then became an enduring and iconic symbol of the suffering of Britain during the Blitz. That night, 500 tonnes of high explosive bombs rained down on Coventry, together with 36,000 incendiary bombs. This surely was total war. This is one of the many target images provided for the briefing of Luftwaffe crews.

GB 739 c
Nur für den Dienstgebrauch

n Bild Nr. 468 L 16

Coventry

**Werk für Flugmotoren- u. Flugzeugzubehörteile
Cornercroft Ltd. Ace Works**

Länge (westl. Greenw.): 1° 30' 50''   Breite: 52° 24' 20''
Mißweisung: — 11° 21' (Mitte 1940)   Zielhöhe über NN 90 m

Maßstab 1:10 560

Genst. 5. Abt. Oktober 1940
Karte 1:100 000
GB 23

GB 739 Werk für Flugmotoren- u Flugzeugzubehörteile   Cornercroft Ltd. Ace Works
1) Große Herstellungs- u Montagehalle u kleinere Werksgebäude   etwa 30 000 qm
2) Verwaltungsgebäude   "   3 000 "

bebaute Fläche etwa 33 000 qm

71

That night, 499 German bombers reached and bombed Coventry. The 500th, a Dornier 17-Z of 6./KG 4, didn't reach its target and was shot down by anti-aircraft fire crashing at Prestwold Hall, Burton on The Wolds, Loughborough. All four men on board were killed and its bomb load scattered far and wide. This was the mangled aftermath of the crash.

Apart from anti-aircraft guns and night fighters another form of defence sometimes claimed its victims: barrage balloons. During the day, the balloons could often be seen by pilots, and they would be forced to fly higher, above them, to avoid their lethal cables. At night, the balloons were mostly invisible and this was the aftermath when a Heinkel 111 of 1./KG 26 flew into a balloon cable over Essex during the early hours of 20 November 1940. The aircraft broke apart and fell onto Beckton Marshes at Jenkins Lane killing all five men on board.

It was also on that same night that another form of defence, slightly more 'high-tec' than balloon cables, came into play: Airborne Interception Radar. An AI equipped RAF Beaufighter of 604 Squadron, piloted by Flt Lt John Cunningham, locked onto a target that night and brought it down at East Wittering in West Sussex. Two of the crew of the 3./KG 54 Junkers 88 baled out safely; a third man landed on his parachute in the sea and drowned; the fourth was found dead in the wreckage, which buried itself deeply in the ground on impact leaving little for RAF investigators to examine. To hide the existence of AI radar, Flt Lt Cunningham was described by the news media as having exceptional night vision. They dubbed him Cat's Eyes and he became a very successful night fighter pilot of the Blitz.

There was little left when another Junkers 88, this time of 8./KG 77, was hit by anti-aircraft fire and crashed at West Stifford, Essex, at 02.15 hours on 9 December 1940 where it dived into the ground at high speed killing all four men on board. The bomber's target had, again, been London's dockland.

It was Manchester that was the target for this Heinkel 111 of 3./KG 55 shot down by a Defiant of 141 Squadron flown by Plt Off J G Benson and Sgt F Blain on 22 December 1940, as a bloody year drew to its close. The wreckage fell into the garden of a property called Underwood House at Etchingham in East Sussex with only one man jumping by parachute and surviving, landing in a tree at Rudyard Kipling's nearby home, 'Batemans', and taken **POW**.

The year ended with a virtual fire storm that raged around the City of London and all but engulfed St Paul's Cathedral. When it was over, the cathedral stood almost alone in a wilderness of rubble and ash. Even those buildings still standing were mostly burned out shells.

Chapter 3
New Year, Same Story

The New Year brought no respite from almost nightly attacks, and as those below huddled in shelters and underground stations an almost endless procession of bombers, on some nights at least, pounded away mercilessly. There seemed to be no respite for attackers or the attacked, although by now the RAF was just starting to get its night fighting defence capabilities better organized and the first 'kills' by radar-equipped night fighters were beginning to mount. No longer were the Luftwaffe having it entirely their own way, and what we were seeing was the start of a really very effective night fighting system that would evolve in the defence of Great Britain across the coming years of the war. However, it had long been apparent that the dark of night was the best means of defence and that daylight attacks were too costly. For the British public, though, there was something doubly terrible about attacks by night and the fear that night itself, especially in a black-out, inevitably brought. However, and although the British public could not know it, there was some respite in store for them as, gradually, the heavy Luftwaffe attacks began to ease, before they almost faded away in the early spring of 1941. The reason was simple; Hitler had turned his sights eastwards and on Russia. Once Hitler had launched Operation Barbarossa the major part of the Luftwaffe bomber force was focussed there and, at last, some relief was found on the British home front.

It had been a terrible few months, and became a time that has since been engrained in British consciousness, folklore and legend. It even spawned an expression still in use today; 'Spirit of the Blitz', a term encapsulating the steadfast ability to face up to anything that the attacks of 1940/41 engendered.

Whilst the Blitz had drawn to an end, though, the attacks were not over entirely. The Luftwaffe would yet be back to terrorize the British population.

One of the first Luftwaffe losses of the New Year involved this Dornier 17-Z crew from 6./KG 2 who failed to return from a night sortie to bomb Liverpool on 2 January 1941. No trace of them was ever found and it was presumed that their aircraft had crashed into the Irish Sea.

When this Dornier 17-Z of 4./KG 3 was sent flaming vertically into the ground it had become the first victim of a remarkable night fighter pilot, Plt Off R P Stevens who would later be awarded the **DSO** and **DFC**. He was a Hurricane pilot with 151 Squadron and truly was a 'Cat's Eyes' pilot, relying on nothing more than exceptional night vision as he stalked enemy raiders in his black-painted Hurricane. The crew of this Dornier had no chance to escape and the wreckage was found the next morning, buried deeply in woodland at Hartswood, near Brentwood in Essex.

Flt Lt Richard Playne Stevens DSO DFC, night fighter pilot extraordinaire, poses by his all-black Hurricane of 151 Squadron. Stevens was the highest scoring night fighter pilot of the Blitz, accounting for twelve Luftwaffe bombers – all of them tracked using nothing more than his remarkable night vision. Stevens was eventually killed whilst stalking a German bomber as it went into land at its base of Glize Rijen in the Netherlands on 15 December 1941.

Southampton, another vital port, became a further night target for the Luftwaffe's Blitz bombers and on the night of 19 January 1941 this Heinkel 111 of 1./KG 1 was hit by anti-aircraft fire over Shoreham in West Sussex. The crippled aircraft crashed not far away at Wyckham Farm, Steyning, and disintegrated in a fireball across several fields. The captain of the aircraft, Hptm Graf zu Castell-Castell and his four crew members were all killed. Here, the army guard have stacked their .303 rifles against the battered and heat blistered tail section of the Heinkel.

The disintegration of the Heinkel was total, with but few sections left that even remotely resembled ever having been an aircraft.

While victories claimed by RAF night fighters were on the increase it also seemed that Anti-Aircraft Command was getting its shooting eye in as more and more German bombers fell to their guns. However, it was the gunners of the Royal Navy who accounted for a Junkers 88 of 8./KG 30 on 26 January 1941 at 16.00 hours off Brightlingsea, Essex, when the guns of **HMS** *Wallace*, *Reids* and *Fisher Boy* engaged the raider, sending it into the sea. There was only one survivor. Here, the two successful RN gunners pose with one of their artillery shells and a recovered portion of the enemy aircraft.

Not every Luftwaffe raider that came down over the British Isles during the night Blitz arrived in such a smashed up state as those that are mostly depicted in the previous pages. During the early hours of 16 February 1941 this Junkers 88 of 8./KG 1 became lost and short of fuel when returning from an attack on Liverpool and landed, wheels down and with its landing lights illuminated, on the flare-path at RAF Steeple Morden in Cambridgeshire. On touching down one of the wheels collapsed, but the aircraft was otherwise intact and the crew were taken prisoner of war, unhurt. The aircraft later ended up as a source of spares for other aircraft of the type that had been captured by the RAF and used for evaluation flying. In this photograph, the Rt. Hon W J Jordan, High Commissioner for New Zealand, is shown the bomber during his visit to the station to see **RNZAF** personnel. Other German aircraft arrivals that night, and the next day, were rather less intact.

This was an aircraft that had been on its way to Birmingham that same night when Flt Lt John Cunningham intervened and claimed his third nocturnal victory, bringing this Heinkel 111 down in flames at Luscombe Farm, Harberton, in Devon. All four of the crew from 7./KG 27 were killed when the bomber ended up incinerated and broken apart across the fields. Night camouflage has been hastily and roughly applied over the day colour scheme, with black distemper painted over the swastika, fuselage sides and pale blue under-surfaces in order to reduce glare and visibility in searchlight beams. The individual aircraft call-sign 'F' has been roughly painted on the tail. However, the camouflage did not help the crew avoid AI radar detection.

That same night, and much further north, the North East coastline was also getting its share of attention from the German air force, with Heinkel 111s of 6./KG 4 taking part in raids around midnight. One of the unit's aircraft was brought to earth in what can only be described as the most dramatic of circumstances. Hit by anti-aircraft fire the 'winged' Heinkel then struck a barrage balloon cable severing a wing which fluttered down onto the foreshore in South Shields. Meanwhile, the rest of the aircraft spiralled downwards to impact at Bents Park, directly into a crater that had been caused by a parachute landmine that had been dropped there on the night of 21 September 1940. Here, five minutes after the crash, another parachute landmine on board the Heinkel detonated and broke windows as far away as Tynemouth and North Shields. In the explosion, Police Constable Lamb and Auxiliary Fireman Purvis were instantly killed and AFS men Renwick and Wharton so severely injured that they died shortly afterwards at Ingham Infirmary. Also taken to the same infirmary was Ofw Wilhelm Beetz, who had managed to parachute out of the doomed aircraft but had the misfortune to land in overhead trolley bus wires which injured and burnt him to such an extent that he, too, died shortly after. His four comrades perished in the aircraft of which little was left for these RAF men to gather into a rather pathetic heap. The drama behind each of the images in this book is sometimes difficult to comprehend when viewing what were often 'posed' photographs.

Further south, and London was again under attack the next night when a Beaufighter of 219 Squadron found a Dornier 17-Z of 3./KGr606 east of the city and sent it flaming into the ground at Oakley Court, Bray, close to Windsor. All four crew were able to abandon their shot up aircraft and left it to smash itself to pieces within sight of Windsor Castle.

Thus far, we have seen aircraft downed as a result of anti-aircraft fire, barrage balloons and night fighters but on 18 February 1941 another defensive measure brought down a German attacker. This time, it was a device called the Parachute and Cable, or **PAC**. This was a system that fired multiple rockets trailing steel cables with parachutes attached. They were designed to snag over-flying aircraft at low altitude. Primarily, the devices were used as defensive measures at **RAF** airfields and this Heinkel 111 was 'snagged' by **PAC** over **RAF** Watton, Norfolk. The aircraft had been on an early morning sortie looking for a convoy of ships that had been reported in the area of The Wash, but when its navigational equipment failed and the crew couldn't find any shipping they dumped their bombs and turned for home, flying at low level because of the bad weather. Unfortunately for the five airmen their course happened to take them directly over the **RAF** airfield at Watton and, now down to 100ft, they presented a perfect target for the **PAC** apparatus. Caught on one of the wings by a cable, the aircraft was disabled and made a good forced landing at Ovington in Norfolk shortly before eight o'clock in the morning. Here, a party from the **PAC** unit are interested in the impact marks from their cable that had sliced into the port wing.

This close-up of the tail shows the roughly applied black night camouflage as well as the remotely controlled MG17 machine gun protruding from the tail that was designed to counter RAF attacks from directly astern. A parachute can be seen on the ground and is being inspected by an RAF officer. This was the 'chute attached to the steel cable which brought the Heinkel down.

Avonmouth was another target for the Luftwaffe force. It was another solitary day raider that came to grief near there on 22 February 1941. The aircraft was a Heinkel 111 from 4./KG 27 and possibly engaged in mine-laying operations when the single shot fired from a 3.7 inch gun of 'B' Troop, 236 Bty, 76th Anti Aircraft Regiment at Portishead scored either a remarkably lucky or skilful direct hit. There was a huge mid-air explosion and the Heinkel plunged into the mud flats off St George's Wharf. One man, Lt Rusche, managed to escape by parachute but the other four were killed with two of them never being located in the wreckage. Here, soldiers struggle in the deep and glutinous mud whilst a local boatman has found his personal trophy: one of the Heinkel's machine guns.

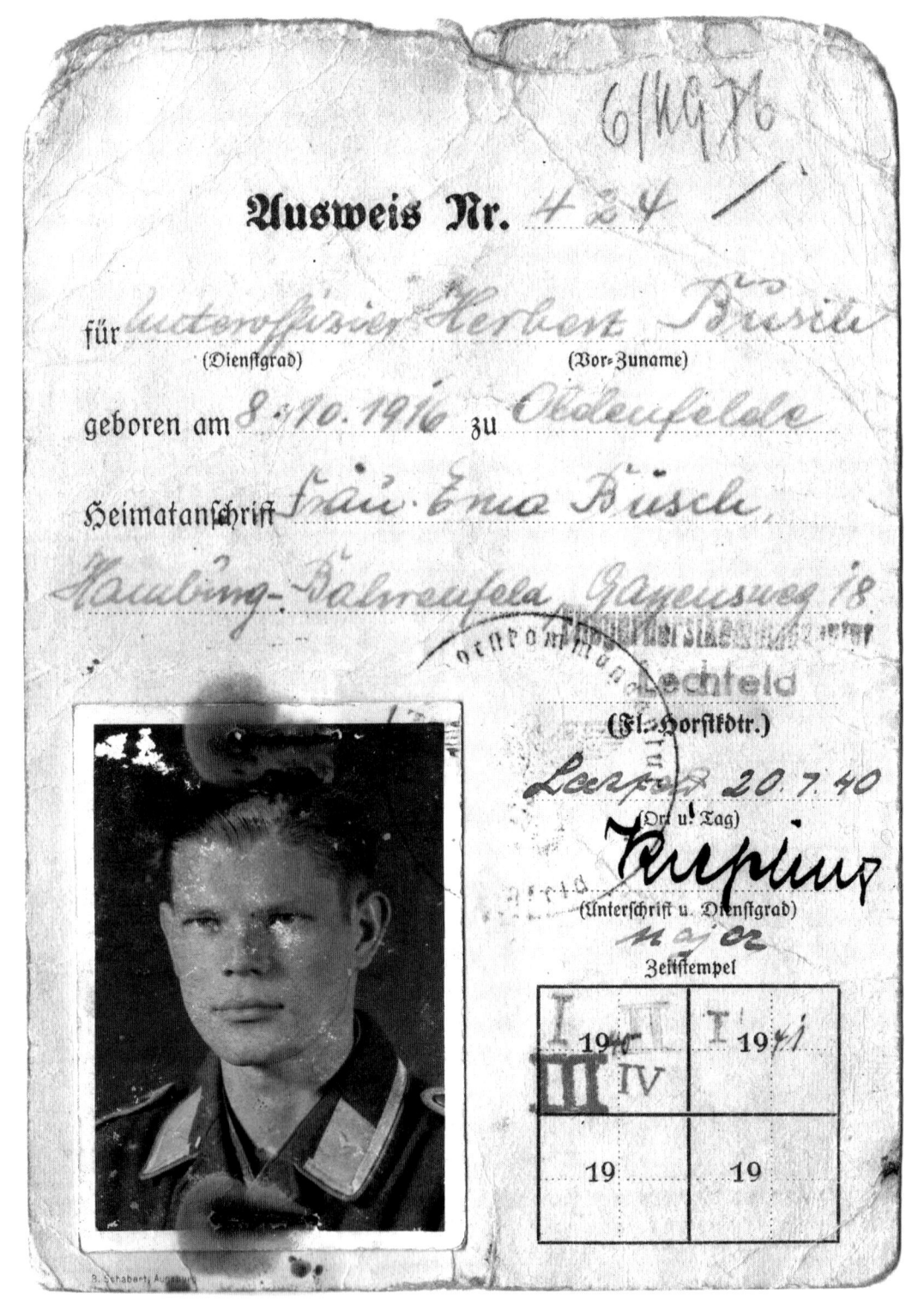

Although the German fliers were the enemy, poignant finds like this Ausweiss (pass) for Ofw Heinrich Busch that was discovered at the scene of a Junkers 88 shot down at Kingston Deverill in Wiltshire bring home the tragedy of such events, with the finder remarking: 'He was somebody's son'. Busch was one of three men killed in a 6./KG 76 machine that had been destroyed by a Beaufighter of 604 Squadron while on a sortie against Portsmouth.

It was again Liverpool that was on the Luftwaffe target list for the night of 12/13 March 1941. One of the aircraft on that sortie was the Heinkel 111 of 5./KG 55 flown by Stabs Fw Karl Brüning that was hit over Sussex by a Defiant night fighter of 264 Squadron with Fg Off Desmond Hughes and Sgt Fred Gash claiming another of their many night victories. The aircraft was inbound to its target when it was set on fire and two out of the four crew were hit and badly wounded. Brüning ordered the other unharmed man to throw out the injured men and open their parachutes as it seemed their only chance. He then held the aircraft as steady as he could before he jumped himself, after leaving time for his men to be clear. As it turned out, Brüning would be the only survivor. This was the wreckage the next morning at Ockley in Surrey. At least one unexploded bomb from it was buried deep underground and not discovered until 1978 when the 500 kg device was dealt with by a Royal Engineer Bomb Disposal (EOD) unit.

St. Fw Karl Brüning, pilot of the Heinkel brought down at Ockley.

Fw Alexander Dussel, who fell dead with an unopened parachute at Holbrook Park, Surrey.

Fw Konrad Steiger and...

Ofw Willi Weisse, also killed in the crash.

The next night, and not far away at Smokehouse Farm, Shipley, another raider was downed over West Sussex during a sortie to Southampton, with a Beaufighter of 219 Squadron again the victor. This time Sgts Clandillon and Doidge were the victorious crew. All four of the 7./KG 26 Heinkel 111 crew were on board as the bomber disintegrated over and around the farm with much of the debris hitting outbuildings and the farmhouse itself, leaving Uffz E Hermann, Uffz Graf Calice, Gefr L Schmid and Ogefr W Kallert dead.

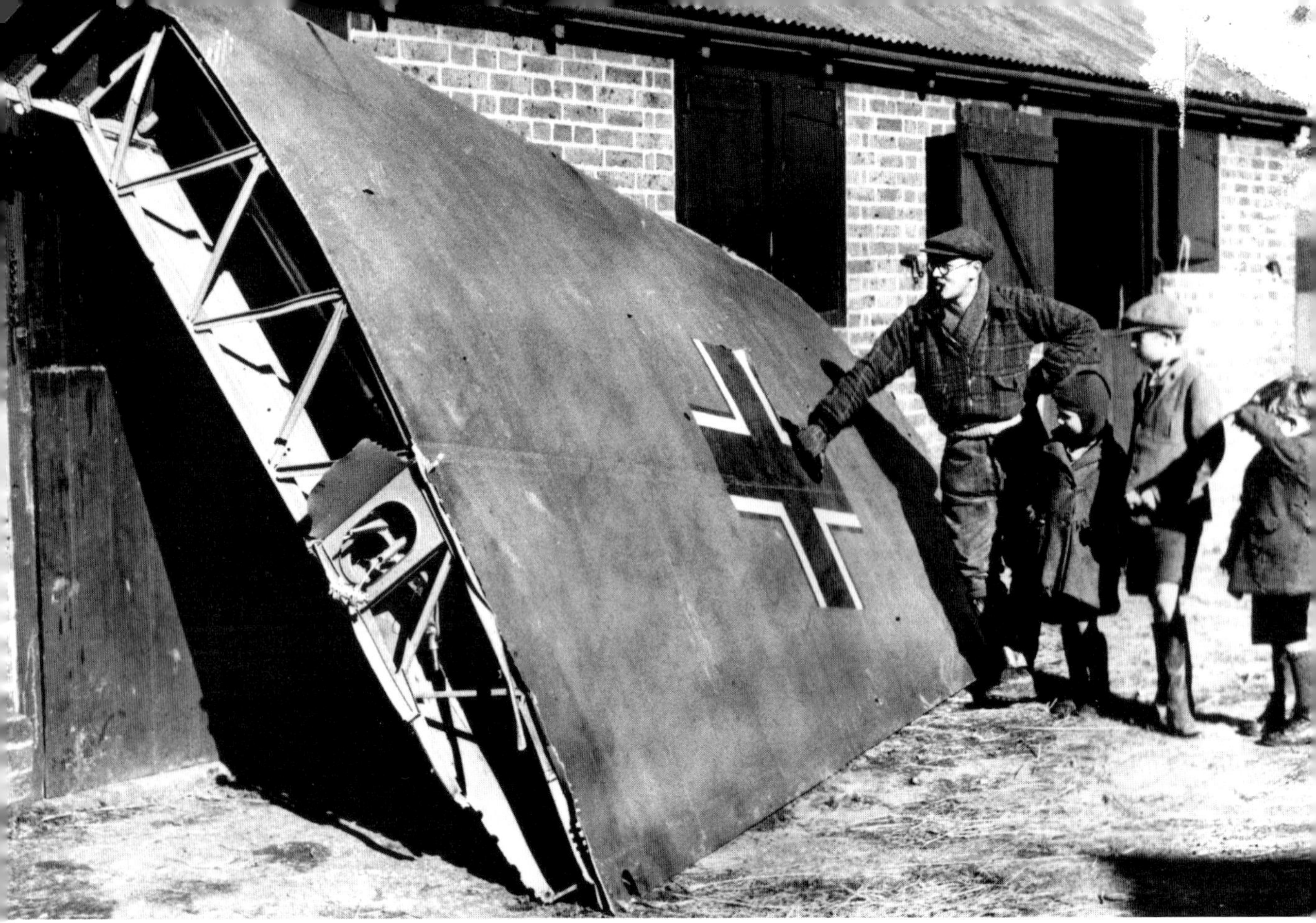

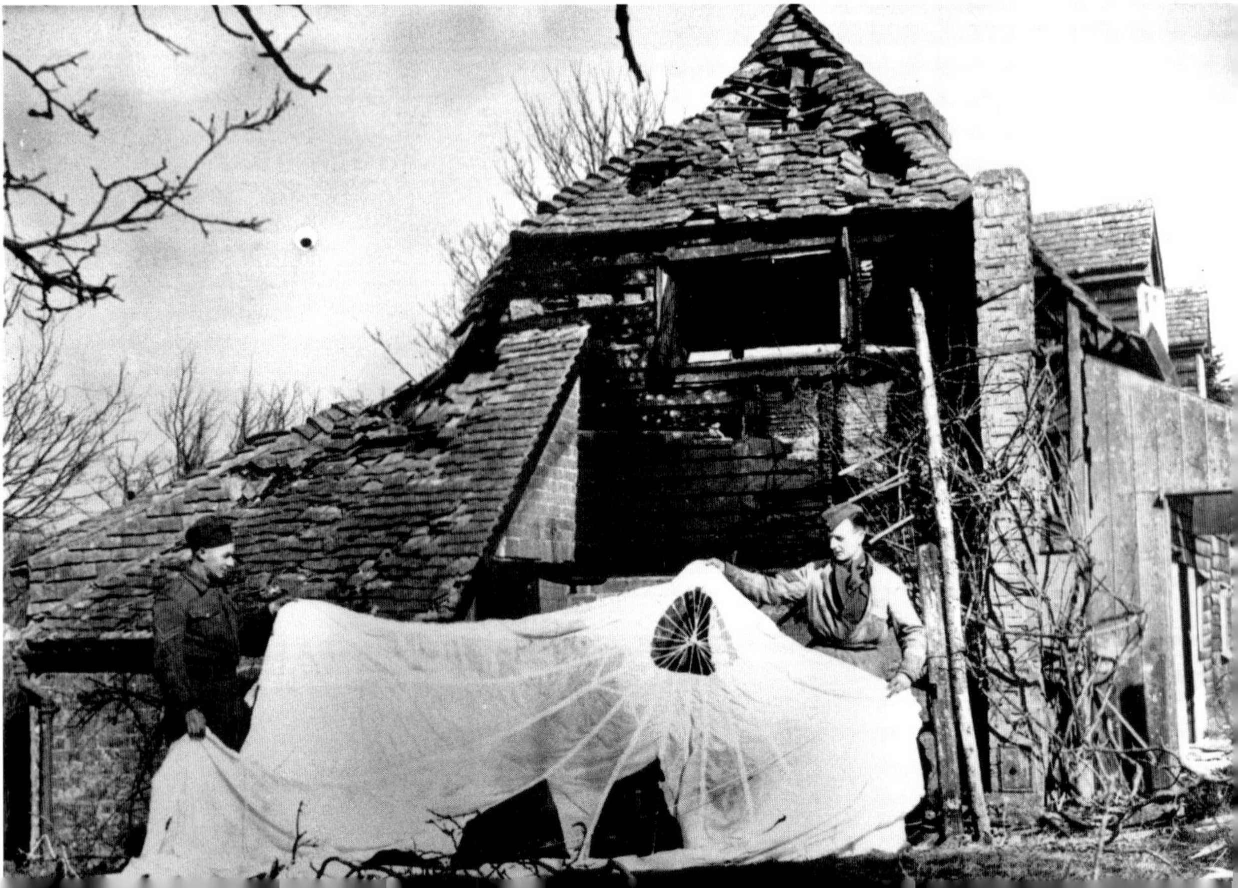

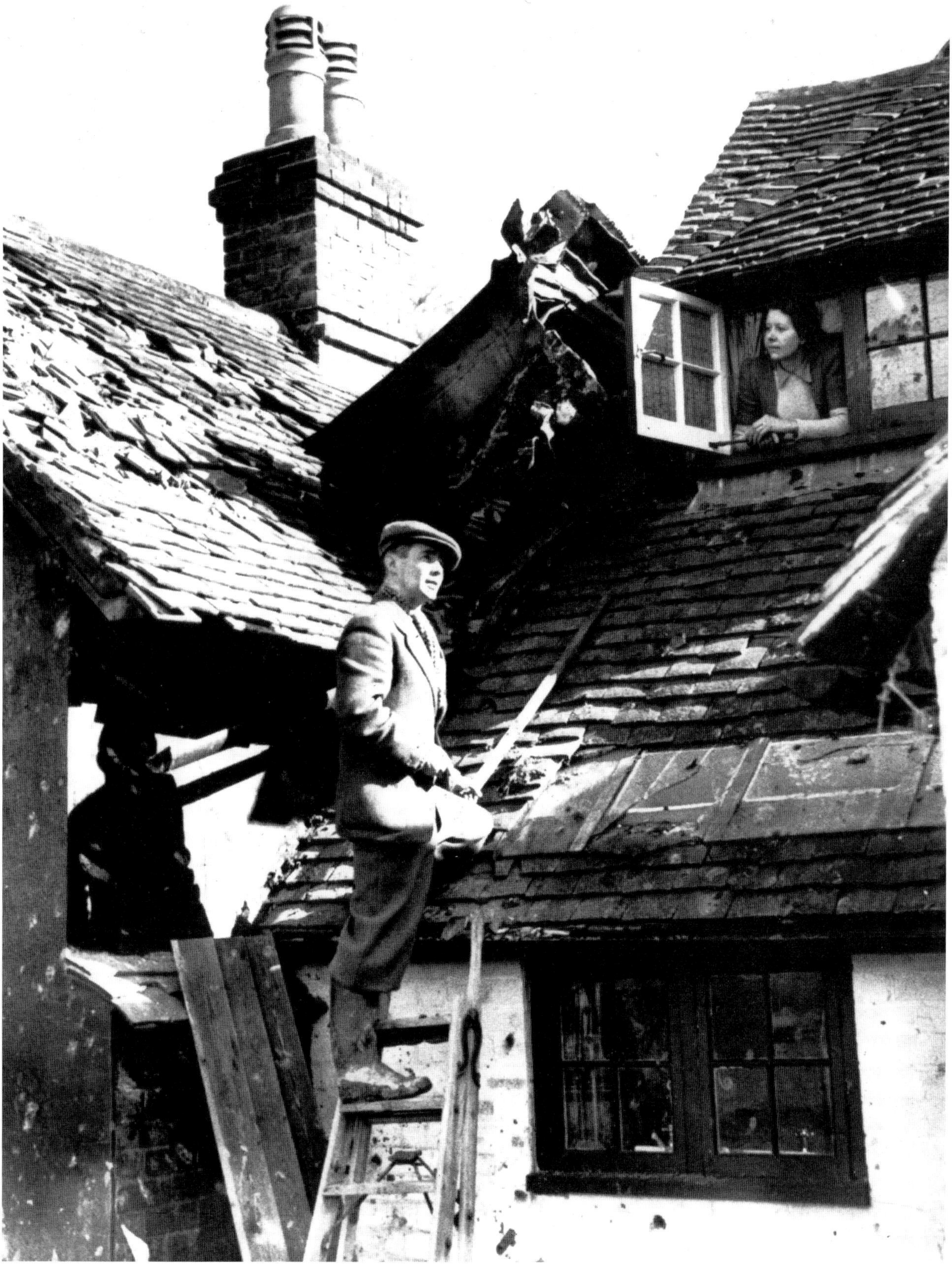

Again, the dangers posed by daylight sorties flown by singleton Luftwaffe bombers over the British Isles during this period was amply demonstrated when this Junkers 88 was shot down by two Hurricanes of 238 Squadron flown by South African Flt Lt E J 'Teddy' Morris and Czech Sgt Frantisek Bernard shortly after mid-day on Sunday, 23 March 1941. The aircraft was operated by 4./KG 77 and three of its crew, Oblt Lode, Uffz Waraczinski and Ofw Billesfeld were taken prisoner. Uffz Wallner had been killed in the fighter attack. At some personal risk, local photographer Harold Petty took this picture at Parsons Farm, Poling, and later had it signed by the two victorious fighter pilots who visited the scene of their victory.

The war was not quite over for Oblt Lode's Junkers 88, though. Removed initially to a scrap processing depot the fuselage was later exhibited at a War Weapons Exhibition at Brighton's Corn Exchange where it attracted much interest and curiosity from the general public who were keen to see a 'Nazi Raider' up close. There was much morale boosting value in such exhibitions, against the damage the Blitz was doing to the fabric of British cities, to industry and to the infrastructure of the British Isles. However, some measure of respite was around the corner as Hitler finalised his plans for Operation Barbarossa, the invasion of the Soviet Union, which would ultimately ease the pressure in the west and on British cities. There was yet, though, one last gasp of the *Blitzkrieg* air assault against Britain to come, during April and May of 1941.

It was over Stockport in Cheshire that one of the first April losses were suffered by the Luftwaffe when a Junkers 88 of 5./KG 54 was sent flaming into Banks Marsh by a Defiant of 256 Squadron flown by Flt Lt D R West and Sgt Adams. Two of the crew managed to escape by parachute, but the other two perished when the Junkers smashed into the marsh. Investigators were faced with a grisly scene as they extricated the mutilated and dismembered bodies of two of the crew from the mangled wreckage. The aftermath of such crashes was often horrendous for those having to deal with the clear-up.

It was Coventry that was again a target on the night of 8/9 April 1941, although this time a number of the raiders were clawed out of the night sky. This was all that was left of the tail unit from a Heinkel 111 of 9./KG 26 that was downed by another RAF Defiant, this time of 264 Squadron, on Vickers Farm at Bendish in Hertfordshire shortly after 10pm. One of the crew died in the wreckage, which included another innovation for rear-facing defence – a grenade launcher. The gutter-like tube of this device may be seen protruding from the very extremity of the fuselage.

Again that night, Flt Lt Richard Stevens was up and hacking down the Blitz raiders. This was all that was left of a 3./KG 55 Heinkel 111 that smashed into the garden of Roe's Rest Farm at Desford in Leicestershire.

And this was Stevens' battle trophy from his shot down Heinkel 111. The swastika-adorned tails of downed aircraft were always attractive souvenirs for victorious pilots, and this one has been embellished with the addition of 151 Squadron's badge in a distinctive white spearhead emblem.

Somewhat further south, and actually in the grounds of Windsor Castle, another KG 55 Heinkel was also shot down that night, and also by an aircraft of 151 Squadron. Unusually, the squadron operated a mix of Hurricanes and Defiants. The Windsor victim, from 8./KG 55, was hit by a Defiant crewed by Flt Lt D F W Darling and Plt Off J S Davidson. Captain of the aircraft was Oblt Jurgen Bartens (although he was not the pilot) and he poses here with his aircraft, sartorially elegant in his riding breeches. Noteworthy is the improvised double MG15 mount on the top turret. Normally, a single machine gun was carried here.

Surprisingly, given its prestigious location, no photographs are known to exist of the crashed Heinkel 111 but there are images of the crew. On the left is **Ofw Franz Vornier** (the pilot) who was killed in the front of the aircraft with Bartens. Incredibly, **Ofw Fritz Pons** (right) survived the crash along with one other man, **Fw Hermann Kubler.** Survival of night time crashes of this nature were extremely rare, especially given the almost total disintegration of the aircraft.

Flt Lt Stevens was not the only person with an eye for a fine trophy that night. This is the three-fishes emblem of 8./KG 55 that was cut from the tail of the crashed bomber and retained by one of those involved in clearing away the wreck and came to light in recent years in a derelict shed. Such tangible relics as these are, now, extremely rare.

And still they came. The very next night, KG 55 were back and this time they were hitting Birmingham. One of their aircraft, G1 + DN of 5./KG 55, was caught by a 264 Squadron Defiant, who were now rapidly upping their 'kill' score. It was another example where there were remarkable escapes of a crew member who remained on board, despite landing at night in wooded and hilly terrain and also striking a substantial tree in the process. The bomber came to rest by a pond at Sheperds Hangar at Busbridge in Surrey at around midnight. Three of the crew, however, were killed.

It was an airman who baled out of this Heinkel 111 on the night of 10 April 1941 who was killed; the pilot who remained on board for a precarious crash-landing amongst anti-glider obstacles survived. The aircraft was a machine of Stab III./KG 26, its pilot Lt Klaus Conrad. This was the burned out hulk of the Heinkel photographed the next morning where it had come to rest on Seaford Golf Course in East Sussex. Anti-glider landing poles and cables can be seen behind the wreck.

Lt Klaus Conrad at the controls of his Heinkel 111.

This was one of Conrad's crew members: Ofw Hermann Platt. The 26-year-old observer on board the Heinkel 111 had jumped from the bomber over the village of Alfriston where the villagers heard his chilling cries and screams as the unfortunate airman tumbled earthwards with an unopened parachute, thus visiting the reality and horror of war on an otherwise sleepy rural community. Platt's body was later located at Rathfinny Farm in Cradle Valley at Alfriston.

Although the majority of incidents recorded in this volume occurred on British mainland cities it should not be forgotten that Northern Ireland also came in for its own Blitz, most particularly the city of Belfast. Late in the evening of 15 April 1944 the Heinkel 111s of 3./KG 53 departed their base at Vitry-en-Artois to attack Belfast and crossed in over Britain's North sea coast at around Flamborough Head. Shortly after this point in its flight it would appear there was some on-board malfunction and fire and the five men on board baled out to become Prisoners of War. Meanwhile, their bomber dived to destruction at Bull Lane Bridge in Huby, Yorkshire. This is the aftermath as soldiers inspect the crumpled German cross that has been ripped from a shattered wing.

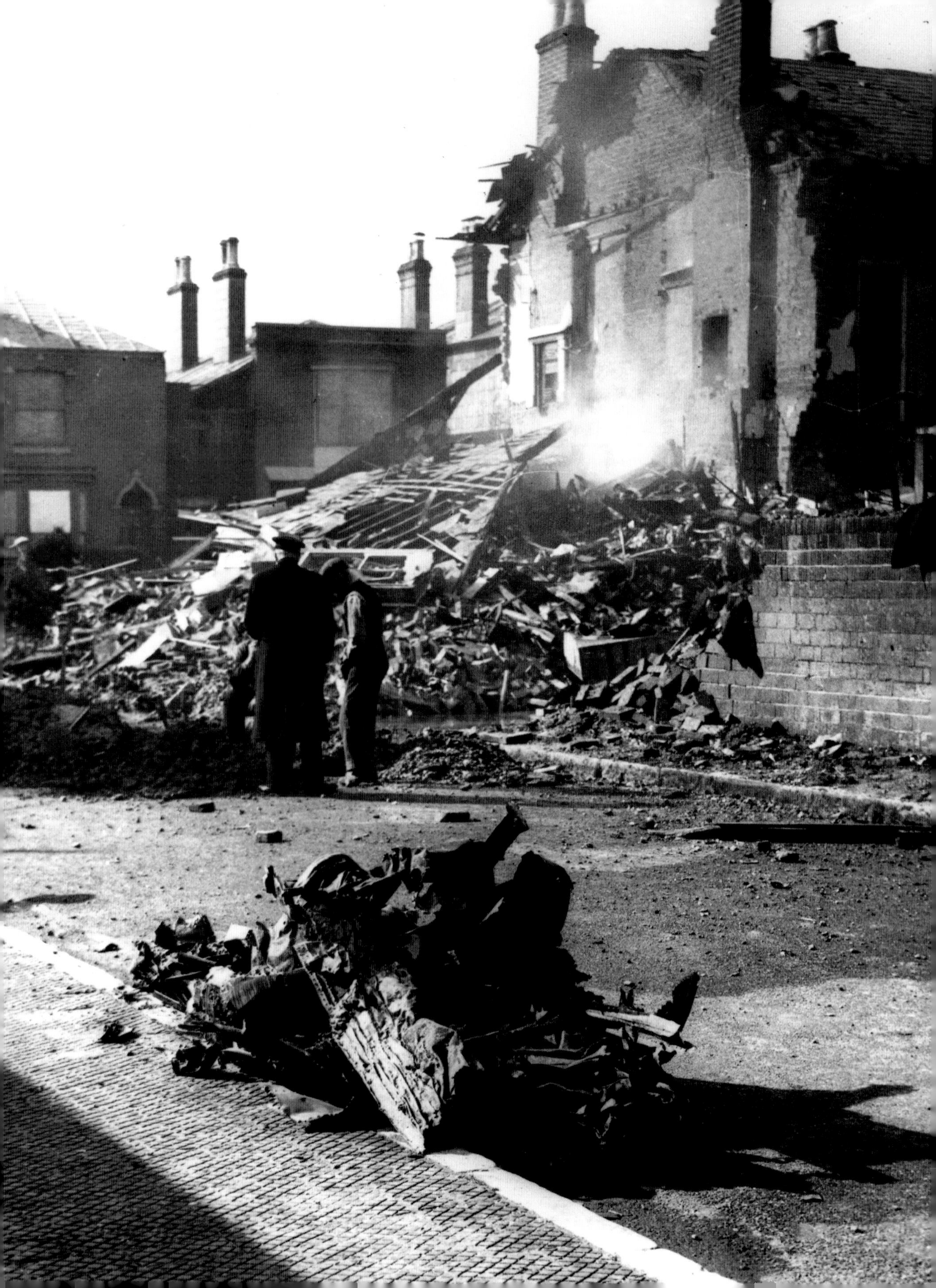

Left: Southampton was again a target on the night of 15/16 April. Again it was a crew of 8./KG 55 who were in the fray and, yet again, it was Flt Lt John Cunningham of 604 claiming a further victim. Unfortunately, the bomber was sent slamming into houses at Padwell Road, Southampton. Two of the crew baled out and survived, but although the other two took to their parachutes one failed to open and the other entangled in a barrage balloon cable. This was the scene the next morning in Padwell Road, Southampton.

The two dead crew members, Oblt Gunther Seidlitz and Fw Franz Hummer, were buried with military honours in Stoneham Cemetery, Southampton, their coffins draped in swastika flags as the Geneva Convention required.

It was now a nightly event that raiders were overhead, British cities took a pounding and bombers were brought down. This was Observatory Gardens at Campden Hill, Kensington in London on the morning of 17 April 1941. Here, civilians and soldiers inspect a large section of wing from a Junkers 88 of 8./KG 77 that broke up after being hit by anti-aircraft fire, the crew abandoning the bomber safely before it fell apart around them.

Another funeral with military honours is afforded the crew of a Junkers 88 that met its end over RAF Thorney Island, West Sussex, after succumbing to anti-aircraft fire during a night attack on nearby Portsmouth the very next night, and crashing to earth at around 02.00 hours on 18 April 1941. The aircraft dived into soft earth on the airfield and became completely buried in the ground, although the remains of Ofw Meier, Uffz Dietzel, Uffz Rothenspieler and Ofw Hocke were retrieved for burial in the churchyard at St Nicholas Church, Thorney Island.

Continuing the nightly routine, yet another Junkers 88 was brought down over southern England on the night of 19/20 April 1941. This time it was a machine of 1./KG 76 that had been hit by anti-aircraft guns at Brooklands after a massive night raid on London. The aircraft went into a screaming vertical dive at full power, and this was the result. The scene looks more like a bomb crater, but is in fact the impact of a German bomber. Only a deep hole, oily water and tiny pieces of debris mark the passing of another four German fliers. The raid had been ordered by Hermann Göring to 'celebrate' Hitler's birthday with an epic 1,000 tons of bombs to be dropped on London in one night, making it the heaviest night of the Blitz. However, the birthday celebrations did not go exactly as planned for Fw Burkhart, Ogefr Scheithauer and Ofw Haselsteiner who lay dead in the corner of an English field at the appropriately named Slaughter Bridge in Slinfold, West Sussex.

Just occasionally there was a return to fighter-bomber attacks against south east targets during this period of all-out Blitz. A case in point was the shooting down of a Messerschmitt 109 of 2./JG 52 over Rye in East Sussex after the pilot, Ofw Gunther Struck, had aimed his bomb at the town's railway station. He was caught by two patrolling Spitfires of 92 Squadron up from RAF Biggin Hill, and baled out into captivity. In 1944, whilst in captivity in Canada, Struck feigned mental illness. He was declared incurably ill and repatriated to Germany where he became a test pilot for the Messerschmitt company. On 21 September 1974 the wreckage of his Messerschmitt was uncovered at Blackhouse Farm. Here, the remarkably well preserved tail unit emerges from the marsh.

This was another victim of Flt Lt John Cunningham's prowess as a night fighter pilot. It is the Heinkel of 9./KG 27 downed en-route to bomb Liverpool and crashing at Wheatsheaf Farm, Corton Denham, on the night of 3 May 1941, and resulting in the death of Fw Albert Amode. The aircraft (1G+IT, W.Nr 1482) is shown here at its base in Rennes, France. The lamp-black under-surfaces are clearly evident in this image.

Another remarkable escape for a German crew crash-landing in their bomber at night time, on this occasion at around 23.30 hours on 4 May. All four men of 6./KG 54 survived when their Junkers 88 was shot down in yet another victory by a Beaufighter of 604 Squadron. The aircraft had been on a mission to bomb Torquay, but ended up against an earth embankment near the Seven Stars Inn at East Burton, Dorset.

When a Heinkel 111 of 9./KG 26 was shot down by a 219 Squadron Beaufighter at around 11 pm on 3 May it ended up crashing into the local corporation scrap yard at Eastergate, near Arundel in West Sussex. The original newspaper caption to this photograph stated: 'It is impossible to tell the bomber from the other junk!' Two men survived after abandoning the aircraft, but another two men died here.

In this second photograph of the same incident it is certainly difficult to distinguish between bedsteads and bombers!

The story behind the almost perfect night-time belly landing of a 6./KG 55 Heinkel 111 at Long Riston during the early hours of 9 May 1941 is a truly remarkable one. Tasked to bomb the steel works at Sheffield, the crew found themselves engaged by a Defiant of 255 Squadron. On its first attack the Defiant killed the pilot, Fw Gerhard Enden, and set fire to the port engine. In a second burst of fire the starboard engine was put out of action and the crew prepared to bale out. In his attempts to leave the aircraft, the observer Fw Heinrich Müller (flying his 45th mission) lost his parachute when it accidentally opened in the fuselage. This left him with no alternative but to try to land the aircraft and he heaved the dead pilot from his seat. Incredibly, he managed a very successful landing. Despite it being at night, having no qualification as a pilot and with both engines out of action it was an astonishing piece of airmanship – with a good dollop of exceptional luck thrown in too! Of the other two men, one died when his parachute failed to open because he was too low when leaving the aircraft. Another man, Fw Georg Schopf, broke his neck when he left the aircraft at only 980 ft. Remarkably, he too survived. Again, an otherwise ordinary photograph of a belly landed bomber hides a far from ordinary story.

Although the Blitz was gradually drawing down, in terms of Luftwaffe resources that were to be committed to the assault on Britain, it could not have seemed so to those still on the receiving end and on the night of 10/11 May 1941 there were still widespread attacks. But the raiders did not get off scot-free: one was this Heinkel 111 which crashed close to houses at Station Road, Withyham, in East Sussex with only one survivor, Lt Martin Reiser, who had jumped with his parachute.

Again, it was a **KG 55** Heinkel 111 (this time of 9./KG 55) that came to grief at quarter to one on the morning of 11 May 1941, falling to earth at Rumbush Farm, Earlswood, near Birmingham. The aircraft had in fact been tasked to attack an aluminium works in the city but got caught in a searchlight. As the pilot tried to evade the probing beams he flew low over the searchlight site and was further dazzled as the lights were directed to deliberately blind him. The searchlight party opened fire with light machine guns and the bomber crashed immediately afterwards and broke up. One of the crew had been hit in the head by a bullet and had died instantly, while two others had died as a result of the impact. A fourth man, Gefr **Budde**, was found staggering around the scene with his clothes on fire and a bullet wound in his leg. Budde eventually fell into a water-filled ditch which extinguished the flames and doubtless saved his life. Here, a soldier of the 380 Searchlight Bty, 45 Searchlight Regt, guards the tail of the Heinkel which has a variation in its camouflage from the more usually seen night-black finish.

Battersea Power Station, such an iconic and obvious target, was singled out for attention as part of a massive two-wave assault on London on the night of 10/11 May 1941; 300 bombers in the first wave and 147 in the second. During that first wave a Heinkel 111 of 1./KG 28 was caught by night fighters and the entire crew baled out and were captured. The bomber broke up and fell around Beehive Lane at Galleywood near Chelmsford in Essex, with one of the detached engines actually falling into the lane itself.

The rear fuselage, meanwhile, fell onto the edge of a nearby orchard where it is examined by soldiers.

A nearby garden was the final resting place of the other engine and a jumble of other debris.

One of the last aircraft brought down over the British Isles in the period generally recognised as 'The Blitz' was a Heinkel of 7./KG 55 – a bomber group which had taken many casualties in the assault on Britain. This aircraft was sent diving into the ground on the South Downs at Sompting, West Sussex, after being blasted from the sky by a Beaufighter of 219 Squadron. The bomber was en-route to its target and had its full bomb load on board when it struck the ground. The aircraft exploded violently, blasting a huge crater and killing the four crew. This was all that was left and again, typically, it is the battered tail section. However, not all of the bombs had exploded...

Ref. Area. WD/VS
Div.
H.Q. Ref.

AIR RAID INCIDENT

Borough, U.D. or Parish ...WORTHING... Date ...17th May, 1941... Time ...00.02 hours...
Number of Exploded Bombs ...—... H.E. ...—... I.B. ...—... O.B. ...—... G.

UNEXPLODED BOMBS

Number and type ...H.E. — 2.... Map reference(s) ...See overleaf...
Date and method of disposal ...See overleaf...
Time and date Control or Sub-Control notified of disposal ...

ROADS CLOSED

—

Description of road(s) blocked or closed ...

Map references ...
Approximate length closed ... Probable duration ...
Cause of Closure ... Diversion ...

Map references ... Whom notified ...
Date road re-opened ... Whom notified ...

CASUALTIES

Killed ...FOUR... Injured Seriously ...—... Injured Slightly ...—...

This is the Sussex Police ARP Incident card recording the crash and noting the presence of two unexploded bombs.

(REVERSE OF CARD)

Detail of Incident referred to overleaf

(To be in tabular form as far as possible, showing locations, principal damage, casualties, etc.)

At 00.02 hours on the 17th May, 1941, an enemy Heinkel 111 crashed on the Borough of Worthing, map reference 585265. The 'plane was destroyed by fire, and the four members of the crew were killed. Two bombs, which the plane had been carrying, and which were found U.X. in the wreckage, were disposed of by the B.D.S. on the 20th May, 1941. No casualties apart from the crew. No damage reported.

Time and Date information received by Police ...

Signature ...

This was the collective grave of the four men at nearby Sompting Parish Church.

Der **Unteroffizier**
                Dienstgrad

der **4./Kampfgeschwader 55**
                Truppenteil

Lorenz Stöger
Vor- und Zuname

ist mit Wirkung vom **1. November 1940** zum

Feldwebel

befördert worden.

                Gefechtsstand, den 1. März 1941.
                Ort   *Datum*

                Kampfgeschwader 55
                Dienststelle

                Name

                Oberstleutnant

                und

                Geschwaderkommodore
                Dienstgrad und Dienststellung

Bestallung

für den **Feldwebel Lorenz Stöger**
Dienstgrad, Vor- und Zuname

der **4./Kampfgeschwader 55**
Truppenteil

Left: Again, a poignant piece of paperwork somehow survived the crash. This was the folded certificate of promotion, dated 1 March 1941, for Fw Lorenz Stoger.

Christliches Andenken im Gebete
an Herrn

Josef Wiederer / Hartmannsreith

Gefreiter u. Bordschütze in einer Flugstaffel

welcher am Dienstag 27 Mai 1941 bei einem Feindflug über dem Seegebiet um England im Jugendalter von 23 Jahren den Heldentod erlitt. Er opferte sein junges Leben für Deutschlands Grösse

Vater Diese harte Stunde,
Deine Liebe gab sie mir
Auch für diese heisse Wunde,
Guter Vater! dank ich dir.

The purpose of this book has been, primarily, to tell the story of the Luftwaffe bombers and their crews who failed to return from bloody missions flown against the British Isles. Appropriate, then, that the final image is of an In Memoriam card for Gefr Josef Wiederer, lost with the entire crew of a Heinkel 111 somewhere in the sea off Gurnard's Head. Once again, this man was from the hard suffering **KG 55**, this time its 4th Staffel.